COLOUR
YOUR ROOM

How to stop being afraid of
colour and use it with style

COLOUR
YOUR ROOM

p

This is a Parragon Book
First published in 2002

Parragon
Queen Street House
4 Queen Street
Bath BA1 1HE, UK

Created and produced for Parragon by The Bridgewater Book Company Ltd.

Creative Director Stephen Knowlden
Art Director Colin Fielder
Designer Johnny Pau
Editorial Director Fiona Biggs
Editors Mark Truman, Sarah Yelling
Photography Alistair Hughes
Picture Researcher Lynda Marshall
Styling & Illustrations Stewart Walton

ISBN: 0-75256-994-5

Printed in China

Contents

Introduction

Colour is everywhere – and we are more aware of it than we realise. We take it very much for granted but imagine what it would be like to only see our world in black and white? We would soon be yearning for some bright colours again. This book will help you look at colours with a decorator's eye and use them to make your home a happier, more comfortable and more stylish place to live. It will also stop you being afraid of colour!

ABOVE **Use of a bold colour on nearly every surface may not appeal to everyone as a decorating option. If the colour is applied with confidence, however, the results can be stunning, and certainly make a strong statement, often reflecting the personality of a room's occupant. This funky purple kitchen is enlivened by the clever use of light on the lime green wall, which reflects on the shiny surfaces.**

Right from a very young age, children are aware of their favourite colours. There is always a favourite red T-shirt or blue jumper that has to be worn over any other piece of clothing. As adults, this awareness is transferred to where we live and the colours we like to be surrounded with. A lot of children, however, also have very strong ideas about what colour they want their bedroom walls to be! The aim of this book is to help you make colour decisions that suit you and your lifestyle best. If, for example, you have a very stressful job, it's no good painting your bedroom bright red – calming aquamarines, lilacs and shades of blue will help provide the right kind of atmosphere.

The first section of the book introduces colour theory and explains the basics. All colours are derived from the three primary colours, red, yellow and blue, from which there are then created the secondary colours of orange, green and violet. There are also hints on creating an illusion – for example, painting your ceiling a darker colour to visually lower it if it is very high – and planning your colour schemes. This is often the most important part as decorating mistakes can be very costly to rectify, and, unless you have unlimited cash, you do need to get it right the first time.

The second section of the book discusses textures and effects, and introduces some projects to try out. It's all very well choosing a colour scheme, but different textures and paint effects can stop that scheme looking flat and dull and will introduce some depth. The third section introduces the concept of colour highlighting, which can also be used to provide interest and diversity in any decorating scheme.

The final section chooses some of the best-known decorating styles from around the world – English Country, Tuscany and Moorish, to name but a few – and shows you how to bring that style into your home. There are felt appliqué curtains, if you fancy bringing a touch of the Romany into your home, and wonderful burnished gold Indian bindi stamps, to add that exotic element to any room. All of these projects – and in fact this whole book – are designed to introduce you to colour and to give maximum impact for minimum effort. So pick a colour you like and get painting!

BELOW **For the typical Tuscan look, use bright colours with a distinctive chalky finish. Ochres, umbers and pistachio green look particularly good here, especially when contrasted with the rich-red rustic cupboard. These chalky Mediterranean paints fade to a wonderful soft colour in the hot sun.**

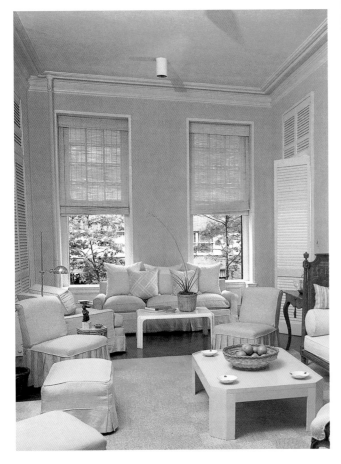

ABOVE **Pink, orange and peach tones can look fantastically lush in the right setting. Here, bright pink walls and lighter pink blinds contrast wonderfully with the warm clotted-cream shades of the upholstery and carpet. The warm ambient lighting mixed with natural light casts a wonderful rosy glow over the whole room.**

Colour and Design

It goes without saying that if we choose the right colour combinations for our homes, then this will undoubtedly help us create rooms that make us feel good. We all have personal colour favourites – you only have to look in someone's wardrobe to discover this. A selection of clothes will be a mixture of instinctive colour preferences and what is currently in vogue. When it comes to decorating, however, the stakes are somewhat higher. Mistakes can be expensive and rectifying them can be very time-consuming. So, it makes sense to take time to plan the kind of colour scheme you want and how it can be made to work in your home. A lot of this comes down to personal taste again, of course, but, if you do have a grasp of colour theory, and know why some colours blend comfortably when they are seen alongside each other, while others seem to vibrate and create visual friction, then you are much more likely to come up with a scheme that really works.

Understanding the colour wheel

Colour breathes life into a home. It can be warm or cool, calm or excite us. Clever use of colour can make small rooms look more spacious or cavernous rooms feel cosy. It can blank out unsightly features and bring the ornate and interesting ones sharply into focus. It has the potential to elevate and enervate all your interior decorating. Never before have home decorators had this much colour choice, and the ranges just keep growing – often leading to more confusion and indecision. How can we select colours that are right for us?

COLOUR THEORY

Knowing some basic colour theory will help you to make colour choices that go beyond your gut reaction to a colour scheme, although that is also hugely important. Basic colour tricks and rules exist, and it is certainly useful to take some time to understand them, even if in the end you decide to break all the rules. Colour has always been a tool for self-expression!

Three hundred years have passed since Sir Isaac Newton shone pure white light through a glass prism onto a neutral background and was delighted to see a continuous band of merging colour ranging from red through orange, yellow, green, blue and violet. In essence he had captured a miniature version of the rainbow, which is created by light passing through drops of rain, causing the spectrum colours to be projected like a giant colour slide across the sky.

THE COLOUR WHEEL

The colour wheel is the standard way to explain colour mixing by separating the spectrum into twelve different colours. At the centre of the wheel is a triangle divided into three equal sections of the primary paint colours – red, yellow and blue.

These three colours are called primary because they cannot be obtained from a mixture of any other colours. Along with black and white, they form the basis of all other paint colours.

RIGHT **Yellow, red and blue are the primary colours on which the colour wheel is based.**

When colours are arranged as a colour wheel, it helps us to understand their relationships to each other and the different effects that are produced when they are used alongside and opposite each other.

Secondary colours are produced by mixing two primary colours:
- yellow + red = orange
- yellow + blue = green
- blue + red = violet.

Tertiary colours are made by mixing a secondary colour with an equal amount of the colour next to it on the wheel:
- yellow + orange = yellow orange (golden yellow)
- red + orange = red orange (burnt orange)
- yellow + green = yellow green (lime green)
- blue + green = blue green (turquoise)
- blue + violet = blue violet (indigo)
- red + violet = red violet (crimson).

It is also useful to discover how much or how little of one colour is added to another to make a third colour. Try making your own colour wheel.

RIGHT **The colour wheel is composed of primary, secondary and tertiary colours.**

KEY

P Primary colour

S Secondary colour

T Tertiary colour

HOW TO MAKE A COLOUR WHEEL

1 Begin with a large dab each of primary red, yellow and blue paint in the middle of a white plate, with yellow at the top, red lower right and blue in the lower left. These are the **primary** colours and will form the basis of your colour wheel.

2 Now mix an equal amount of primary colour into the one next to it, around the outside of the original three colours. You will produce orange, green and violet. These **secondary** colours fill the spaces midway between each two primaries.

3 Place a dot of each primary colour on the plate rim opposite its central position, and do the same with the secondary colours. Leave a space between each large enough for the **tertiary** colours (made by mixing a secondary colour with an equal amount of the colour next to it on the wheel).

Colour terms

The language used to describe colour includes some specific terms that you may not have come across before unless you have studied art or interior design. The few terms that are explained here are those that are most likely to be mentioned within the context of home decorating. Some specialist terminology will come in handy and make it much easier to communicate your thoughts and ideas about colour when dealing with professionals in the industry.

LEFT **Golden yellow and mauve clash with each other, producing a kind of visual discomfort.**

BELOW **Blue and orange appear directly opposite each other on the colour wheel and are known as complementary colours.**

ADDITIVE COLOUR

This is the colour of light, where adding all the colours together creates white light.

CLASHES OR DISCORDS

This describes two colours of equal intensity, which cause visual discomfort. Think of them as musical harmonies and discords. Designers and artists sometimes make use of this effect to create a disturbance and give the colour scheme an 'edge', and colour clashes were most famously used in the rebellious 1960s – bright orange and shocking pink, for instance, or golden yellow and mauve.

COMPLEMENTARY COLOURS

Colours opposite each other on the colour wheel are called 'complementary'. These are colours of equal intensity. When they are combined in equal proportions they make a neutral grey. When placed alongside each other, they achieve maximum intensity and compete for attention.

ABOVE **In the black and white half of this picture the light foreground and dark background are very clearly defined. In the coloured half the tonal contrasts are not as obvious because the glow from the bright yellow illuminates the wall.**

CONTRASTS

Hue

The simplest contrast to understand is that of hue, which describes the difference between undiluted colours seen alongside each other. The primary colours (yellow, red and blue) are the most extreme example.

Hot and cold

Some colours are hot – red, yellow and orange; some are cold – blue, green and violet. The most extreme hot/cold contrasts are red-orange and blue-green.

Light and dark

Light and dark contrast is clear when you look at a colour and a black-and-white version of the same photograph. Red and green have the same tonal quality and show up as an equal grey. Yellow and violet are the most extreme examples of this contrast (apart from black and white, which are not colours, but tones).

HUE

A hue is one of the pure colours of the spectrum, like red or yellow, and it can be used to describe the

character of another colour – for example, lavender has a violet hue, olive has a green hue or pink has a red hue.

HARMONIES

A harmony is a combination of colours that allows the eye to travel smoothly between them with no sharp contrasts. Colours that are close to each other on the colour wheel will naturally harmonise – yellow, orange and red, for example.

INTENSITY

This describes how much pigment is in the paint. The more pigment there is, the stronger and less diluted the colour will be. Another word used to describe colour intensity is saturation.

NEUTRALS

These are black, white, grey, beige and cream.

SURFACE COLOUR OR PAINT COLOUR

This is colour that is mixed from pigments, where adding all the primary colours together creates black. This is the colour we deal with when decorating, which differs from the colours of light. When all the primary colours of light are combined, the resulting light is white.

TINTS AND SHADES

The addition of white to a colour produces a tint, which we call a pastel colour; and black darkens a colour to produce a shade.

ABOVE **These three blocks are an example of subtle tints and shades. The central colour has been lightened by tinting with white (left) and darkened by adding a small amount of black (right).**

Personal taste

If you were to start with a clean slate and were able to reinvent your personal taste, the result is likely to be as sterile as a hotel room or a room set in a furniture show room. These rooms, designed to make many different people feel at home, always lack the character of personal expression. Taste evolves with us, whether as a result of rejecting our parents' taste or being strongly influenced by fashion or a particular era's decorating style. Our taste in colours also builds up over the years and is developed from an accumulation of influences that go back to childhood.

A BACKGROUND TO YOUR LIFE

Visualise a living room with a white ceiling, pale blue walls, white woodwork and natural polished wood flooring. This is a traditional classic colour scheme, chosen to provide an unobtrusive background for elegant furniture – perhaps some antiques and paintings, and a chandelier. Now place your own furniture in the room and imagine how it will look.

Picture the same room with the skirting and window frames painted a deep turquoise blue and the walls sunshine yellow. Is this more your sort of look? This is an extreme version of a very useful exercise, because the things you already own and love can provide the best clues when you are looking for a new colour scheme.

The front door makes the first statement about who lives behind it, and your colour choice can advertise or conceal your personality. Vivid orange, bright golden yellow or scarlet announce flamboyance and sociability; and deep green suggests a much calmer welcome.

Busy rooms – like family kitchens, where there is a constant flow of traffic and activity – benefit from bold colours and strong contrasts, which add to the room's dynamism. Hallways look inviting in warm yellow or burnt orange, whereas a bedroom is more relaxing if painted a calming green, meditative blue or lilac.

The way your house functions is improved by the colours chosen for rooms and connecting areas.

LEFT **The detail of this fine old chair would be lost if set against a bright patterned wallpaper. Design your colour schemes to flatter the furniture or objects you already own.**

RIGHT **This rough distressed wall finish is a perfect background for a contemporary folding chair. The different textures create a contradiction that gives the image energy. The very old and very new often make good companions.**

Art Deco

In the 1920s the Art Deco style was one of symmetry, stepped shapes, vertical lines and smooth surfaces. The style was influenced by the Cubist art movement and the arrival of the movies and the great ocean liners. Chrome, glass, ceramics, marble and leather were some of the most popular ingredients. This was an era when 'having style' was considered a top priority. This room features a classic 1920s fireplace and a stunning circular ceiling.

COLOUR KEY

1 Cream
2 Plaster pink
3 Warm orange

FOLLOWING FASHION

Decorating has always followed fashion. Fashions used to be dictated by kings and queens and ignored at your peril. Scarcity of certain pigments played a large part in how and where they were used, until the Victorians invented synthetic colour dyes. Initially pigments were made from earth, minerals or plants; some were rare and expensive. Blue and purple are two colours whose rarity ensured that they were reserved for royalty and deity, and they still hold these associations today.

These days we are more likely to be influenced by top fashion designers, whose work often encompasses interiors and home accessories. This cross-over has introduced an aspirational feeling to interior decorating and spawned many magazines. Fashion is fun and, because it is ever-changing, it is also refreshing. The latest colour scheme can certainly bring a drab room right up to date, but it is important to avoid being a fashion victim. Decorating is big business – to keep the tills ringing, paint companies also ring the colour changes every season. But stick to what you like and what suits your room – unless you feel like a change!

Diner-style

The 1950s style is bold and fun. In the 1950s, decorating celebrated the return of colour after the drab war years, and many of the innovations that had focused on the military were at the disposal of designers for the home market. The plastics industry celebrated with coloured laminated surfaces and moulded plastic shapes. Chrome kitchen appliances echoed the shapes of streamlined cars and planes and black and white checked patterns added style.

COLOUR KEY

1 Ketchup red
2 Gloss white
3 Black

FAVOURITISM

We all favour certain colours, and consequently no amount of theoretical knowledge is going to convince someone to paint a room purple if they are of a pastel pink persuasion.

Vive la différence! Each of us is unique, and personal taste varies enormously.

Pattern and texture

 A colourful room without textural contrasts would look strangely sterile. The texture of an object is one of our key descriptive tools, and a surface pattern can be used to enhance a shape or carry a colour scheme. When solid colour seems heavy and overpowering over large areas, a patterned version can give a much lighter feel. The dense texture of a carpet means a plain colour often works well on the floor but would look better in a sheer version for curtains or a patterned wallpaper.

Faux linen: denim blue is a good colour for upholstery.

Faux snakeskin: chenille printed in a python pattern.

Woven chenille: a flat weave fabric with a very soft texture.

Woven check: in harmonious orange, yellow and cream.

Cotton/linen: embodying the English country-house style.

Casbah: this pattern motif works well with a traditional style.

Jacquard weave: a hard-wearing fabric good for upholstery.

Leather: the most hard-wearing of all upholstery material.

Gold chenille: a rich loose-weave chenille with a corded texture.

Woven dobby: fabric that has the look of brushed denim.

Suède fabric: the look of real suède and a smooth texture.

PATTERN

Interior decorating styles follow catwalk fashions, and most of the top clothes designers now also have home ranges that include furniture, carpets, fabrics and paint colours. So it is possible to co-ordinate every area of your life in the style of someone with impeccable design credentials! In real life, few of us would go that far – but it is useful to keep an eye on fashion, where you will find clues to new colour trends. Pattern has been kept to a minimum for a long time, but that is about to change, and this is good for home decorators. Pattern is a great way of introducing more colour into a room.

TEXTURE

The texture of a colour can change its appearance more than you would imagine. Some colours look bland and dead when painted in a matt emulsion. Terracotta is a good example of this, as it only comes to life on a rough rustic surface or when used as a patchy colourwash. Mint green is another example – it looks fresh and fantastic in a chalky finish, but safe and dull in a flat emulsion. Some colours benefit from having a reflective sheen, especially in combination with a contrasting matt colour. Matt chocolate-brown woodwork with a glossy cream wall looks really delicious, and red always looks better with a sheen. The deep green of glass bottles is stunning with light shining through it, but the colour is nothing without transparency and light. Experiment with sample pots if you are unsure about which texture of paint will give the look you're after.

A room style based on a natural palette where there is little colour variation is brought to life by different textures, such as woven wool, linens and cottons, sisal matting, sheepskin, leather, bleached wood and glass. A very little colour will go a long way when a rich variety of textures provides the visual interest.

ABOVE **In this room the chalky texture of the walls has been emphasised by the use of a high sheen paint for the dado rail. Chalk finish paints dry to a paler version of the applied colour and have a soft, powdery surface bloom. Any type of paint can be given a glossy finish by applying a coat of clear gloss varnish.**

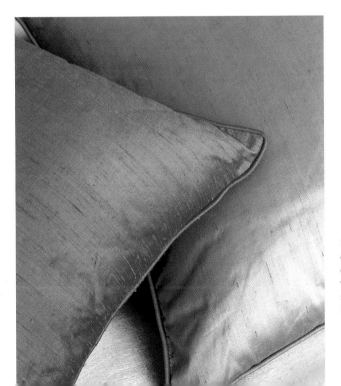

LEFT **Cushions are the easiest way to introduce different textures and colours to a room. Look for cushion fabrics with an obviously contrasting texture to the furniture upholstery, such as these shiny Shantung silks against the unbleached rough linen of the sofa.**

Creating an illusion

Colour can be a magical tool if you have awkwardly proportioned rooms, as often happens when houses are converted into flats. When big rooms are divided up, high ceilings can make them look smaller than they are. This is where clever use of colour comes in useful.

If a room has unusual proportions, colour is the cheapest way to improve it without structural alterations. Light colours reflect the most light, making rooms appear bigger and brighter, while dark colours have the opposite effect.

TRICKS OF THE TRADE

A very high ceiling can be made to look a lot lower if a light colour is used on the walls up to the height where the ceiling would be in proportion with the room, then a dark colour is used above it for the top part of the walls and the ceiling. Fix a chandelier to hang into the room below the dark top section and the high ceiling will 'appear to disappear'. If you prefer not to have a central light, then make a feature of the lighting by using sculptural contemporary lights to create focal points where you choose to have them, or large table lamps that shed pools of light to give a cosy atmosphere. Look out for the new rechargeable coloured balls of light – the charge lasts about four hours, and nobody will ever notice your high ceiling!

A low ceiling will look higher if the walls are painted in a dark colour or papered with a 'busy' patterned paper up to dado rail height, then painted a very light colour above it, including the ceiling. Lighting and colour can help exaggerate the illusion of space. Harness blue's receding quality and use subtle washes of light from uplighters to add the most height, like looking up into a pale summer sky. For a fantastic contemporary design solution, try soft washes of slowly changing coloured light on a white ceiling to turn your low ceiling into an art feature. Specialist lighting shops have the necessary equipment, and they are a lot less rare than they used to be.

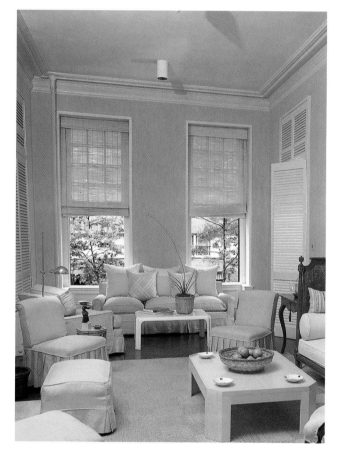

ABOVE **Faced with a room with fine proportions like this one, it would have been a pity to spoil the symmetry by boxing in pipework. The far more sympathetic and successful alternative was simply to paint the pipes to match the background. This works particularly well with a matt paint finish because the shapes don't catch the light.**

LEFT **One way to create a harmonious home is to link the colours of one room with the corridor, stairway or a feature in the next room. Here the staircase is painted to match the woodwork in the foreground and a band of the blue along the top of the skirting or string echoes the room's wall colour.**

OPTICAL ILLUSIONS

• If the room is long and narrow, it can be made to look wider by painting the longer walls with a cool pale green or blue, so that the walls appear to recede. The narrower walls will appear to advance if you paint them in a deep, warm shade of red or red-brown.

• Paint corridors to harmonise with the room colour and remove doors to create a more open-plan sense of space in a small flat.

• Make 'small' a virtue by painting walls and ceilings of tiny rooms in deep warm colours for a wrap-around cosiness.

• Blot out unwanted details like pipework or damaged plaster features by painting them the same colour as the surroundings.

• Add interest to a square plain room by creating optical illusions with blocks of colour. Drop-shadows, stripes or stencilled mouldings can all be used in contemporary or traditional ways.

ABOVE **You can make a low ceiling seem higher by painting the walls in a dark colour and the ceiling in a pale colour or white.**

RIGHT **Painting the ceiling in a darker colour than the walls of a room will appear to reduce the height of the room and provide a more intimate atmosphere.**

Colour and light

The appearance of a colour depends on the quality of the light it is seen in. Most of us share the experience of being unable to tell navy blue from black inside a store but once outside the blueness is revealed by daylight. Every colour can be enhanced, softened or highlighted with lighting. The combination of a warm colour scheme and soft lighting can create a relaxing environment, and cool colours with sharp contrasts and bright directional light can give a dull space an energetic uplift.

GETTING THE LIGHTING RIGHT

The boldest or most subtle colour scheme in the world looks the same in the dark – so it follows that getting the lighting right is absolutely vital. This means making the most of the natural light as well as using the best sort of artificial light for the effect you are after. Anyone who has visited a night club during the day will understand the magic of clever lighting, as daylight reveals what the lighting conceals. If your living room is the children's playroom during the day, then clever lighting tricks can help to create a more sensual atmosphere in the evening. Dimmer switches, uplighters and concealed lights will create soft ambient lighting conditions, and table lamps make pools of light that add intimacy to a room. Task spotlights can be used for 'work' areas such as hi-fi, TV and games consuls. Use small spots to accent flowers, art or any other features.

ABOVE, LEFT **Sunlight streams in through the gap between the muslin curtain and the window frame. The muslin softens the light that would otherwise dazzle in a white room. The floor is painted concrete and the walls whitewashed plaster yet the room has atmosphere created by the combination of a cotton rug, an attractive chair and the quality of the light.**

LEFT **Concealed neon tubes below the wall units illuminate this cool modern kitchen. Kitchens are often too bright but here the task lighting is concentrated on the work surfaces. The light bounces off the one emerald green wall, casting a cool, watery, green light on the whole room.**

LEFT **Rich red walls and a dark rug surround this dining table. The spotlights are all focused on the tabletop, throwing the rest of the room into shadow and creating a sense of intimacy for an adult meal. The high chair in the background gives a hint that this room adopts a very different character during the day.**

BELOW **Yellow is the lightest and the brightest of the primary colours. It glows with reflected natural light and infuses the room with sunshine and warmth. The use of pink in the room beyond has an enticing effect when framed by the yellow.**

A cool, north-facing room can be infused with warmth and light if you paint the walls warm light yellow, and any room will look lighter if you paint walls opposite the windows white or any other very light colour. If the windows are small, the natural light in the room will appear to double if the frame, recess and immediate surround are painted white.

Coloured glass or sheets of adhesive colour film applied to windows can change the room colour during the day. A white room can glow with pink, yellow or green when the sun shines through the glass, only to return to white again when the sun passes. In the same way, coloured lights can be used at night to change the mood and colour of a room. One London hotel has a range of coloured lighting options in every room, so guests can choose the room's colour mood.

Planning colour schemes

The starting point here is inspiration, and this could come from a room style seen in a magazine, a classic period style such as Regency, or the regional colours seen on a holiday abroad. Or it could be a combination of colours on a piece of fabric, in the corner of a painting, in a bunch of flowers, or in a bowl of fruit or sugared almonds – anything at all that pleases your eye and could be translated into colours for a room. Analyse the source of your inspiration to discover which of the colours will create the right mood.

SELECTION FACTORS

If the walls are to be all one colour, then it should work in context with all the above considerations. Lighter and darker versions of the same colour may be a better option, allowing some areas to appear more prominent than others.

Patterned wallpaper could also be used to add texture and variety without introducing another main colour. Bold patterns are back in fashion, and the right ones will certainly bring a room right up to date.

If you decide to base your colour scheme on an historical or regional style, the colour choices will be restricted to particular palettes. The colours simply have to be combined in the traditional way, and success is assured. Everything does not have to be innovative and original, and with colour schemes it is generally better to look at something that works well, then copy it.

Decide upon the main colours for the room. The walls, the ceiling, the floor and the woodwork are the key areas. Unless you are looking to create the illusion of a lower ceiling, then this should be the lightest colour in the room. The wall colour or colours can be either matt or have a slight sheen. The reflective sheen is best for pale colours where you want to increase the light in a room. Matt gives the most sophisticated look. Gloss is an unusual choice for walls but it is practical for hallways and stairways, especially when there are children in the house.

ABOVE **This rustic Mediterranean home is furnished with an eclectic mixture of art and country furniture. The room is whitewashed and the beams have been picked out in the brilliant blue typical of the region. Blue and white predominate for walls and woodwork, but the bright furnishings, pictures and flowers create a much more multicoloured look.**

features exist does not mean that they have to be picked out and contrasted with the wall colour.

Sometimes in a small room a more spacious, expansive effect is achieved by simply painting them the same colour as the walls, using an eggshell or satinwood paint. A large room, however, may benefit from the unifying effect of strong bands of colour at skirting, dado and picture rail height.

FLOORING

A new wooden floor will give any room a very clean, contemporary look, and the cost need not be exorbitant if you choose one of the cheaper laminates. It will provide a good base for colourful rugs, and the 'click' type of floorboards do not require glue and can be easily lifted and relaid elsewhere. If existing wooden floorboards are in reasonable condition, they can be painted or stripped and stained. This style of flooring is popular at the moment, and it can always be carpeted over in the future, so there is nothing to lose.

If new flooring is not an option, then the colour scheme will have to be chosen to take the existing flooring into account. If you have a rust-coloured carpet, for instance, choosing a contrast colour like light turquoise or ice blue for the walls will give you a much fresher, livelier effect than a more conventional harmonious yellow, cream or orange.

ABOVE **Inspiration for planning your colour scheme can come from a wide variety of sources in your environment; make a collection of inspiring objects.**

WINDOW FRAMES

Window frames are conventionally painted in a lighter colour than walls, as this reflects more light into the room. Unless they are an attractive key feature in the room, such as lovely old sashes or huge plate glass windows, the frames look better when kept light and neutral, as colour will make a feature of any defects.

SKIRTING BOARDS AND DADO RAILS

Skirting boards and dado or picture rails in older houses provide an opportunity for horizontal bands of colour to divide the walls in clean lines. Just because these

PATTERNS

If you would like to use a pattern, there are a few basic rules worth considering. Large patterns work best in large areas and small patterns are best suited to small areas where they can be appreciated. A small floral pattern will read as a texture from a distance, whereas a large floral repeat in a small area is far too overwhelming.

Geometric patterns have recently made a big come-back and, as an alternative to hanging wallpaper, a wall can be treated as a giant painter's canvas with stripes, circles and squares of colour.

Making a swatch board

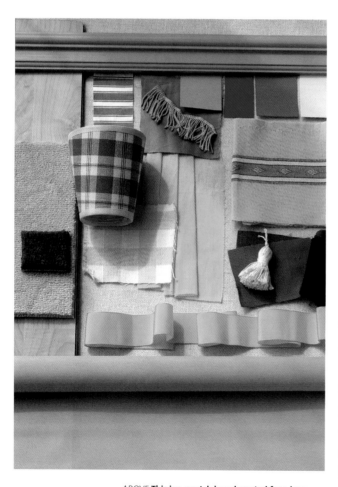

Not only is this a useful exercise, but it is also great fun. It will help you to make the right choices if you are dealing with something tangible. Begin with your source of inspiration, whether this is a scrap of fabric, a postcard or a photograph you took on holiday. Place this onto a white background to isolate the colours. Take it with you to the paint store, and collect sample paint swatches that match, harmonise or contrast with it. Look at several different manufacturers' ranges as the colours vary a lot.

ABOVE This is a swatch board created for a long sunny sitting room with a dining area at one end. The two main colours were used to homogenise the space, and differences in texture defined the areas. A detailed swatch board like this makes it easier to visualise the finished room.

PAINTED SWATCHES

If your budget stretches to it, then also look at specialist ranges where the colours and finishes are often more unusual. Look out for painted swatches, which are far more accurate than the printed versions. If you are sensitive to chemicals, or simply wish to follow an environmentally kinder route, then send away for the 'greener' paint companies' colour cards.

Once you have found your colours, buy sample pots and paint them onto a piece of white board (at least 300mm sq./12in sq.) so you can see what the colour looks like, and whether it is true to the colour card. Placing the board opposite the window, and in a dark corner, will help you judge whether you could go lighter or darker without changing the colour. See what it looks like with things you will not change in the room.

Take the colour swatch with you when choosing fabric, wallpaper and carpets. Get samples of anything you like and put them together on the swatchboard. Once you have carpet, fabric and wallpaper, you will be able to see how the textures affect the colours. Refer back to your original inspiration and compare the colours to the ones that inspired you in the first place. If you haven't managed to find the right colours and you have time for more research, keep looking. There are more paint companies out there than you think, and it is usually the smaller, more specialist shops that deal in the desirable, unusual colours.

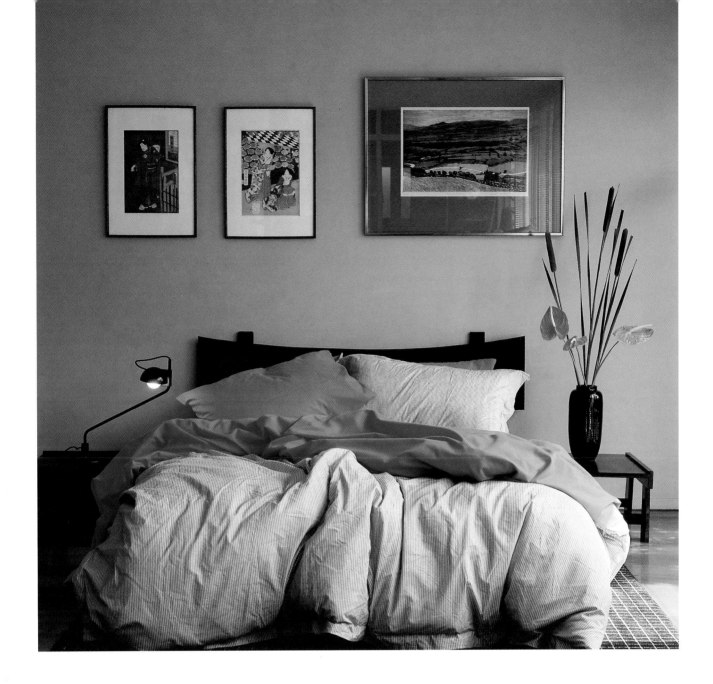

BRINGING IT ALL TOGETHER

When you have established your basic colour scheme (walls, ceiling, flooring, woodwork, soft furnishings), you can experiment with other textures, patterns and colours for the accessories. It may be that a very muted colour scheme needs a vibrant accent of colour to set it off, or conversely that a gaudy background cries out for a plain neutral rug or sofa. A newly painted bare room can look unbearably bright until all your possessions are back in place. Walls can be broken up with pictures, lighting and shelves, and key wall colours can be picked up on small items like vases, picture frames, cushions and lampshades to create a more unified colour scheme.

ABOVE **A beautiful room, which demonstrates successful use of colour in interior design. The walls are painted a warm yellow-green, and the same shade appears in the landscape painting. The pictures are thoughtfully hung along a level base line. The natural yellow pine floor is polished to a high sheen to reflect and enhance the natural light, and the rug frames the sleeping area. The simple off-white grid pattern of the rug diffuses the intense indigo blue, creating another level of low-key pattern and colour interest. The bed linen in a contrast of muted grey/white stripe and hot salmon pink creates a seductive focal point. The spiky bullrushes and the contemporary black lamp perfectly balance each other's shapes. The room is a wonderful example of harmony, balance and style.**

Textures and Effects

The appearance of colour can be completely changed by the introduction of texture. Texture can add depth to a decorating scheme and enhance the impact of different colours. Up until now – and the recent decorating revolution – thick wallpapers and embossed plaster patterns were only used if you had a problem with your walls and wanted to cover it up. An applied texture like this is now seen as a serious design statement, and can add bags of character to a new house or enhance the original features of an older property. You can use different coloured and textured paints, natural materials, such as split bamboo, raffia and linen, and even a cosy fabric like fleece applied directly to the walls. All you need to do is get the colours right, and you're away.

Texture

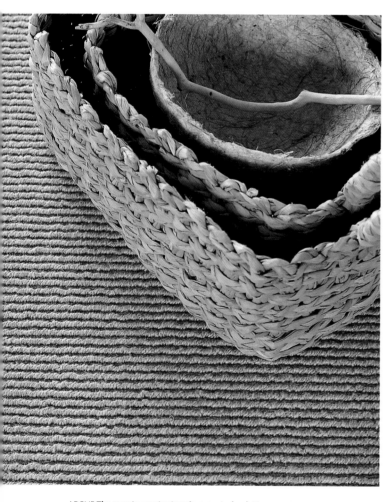

The way we choose and combine different textures for decorating is as much affected by trends as by our colour choices. Felt, once used only as a protective barrier, underlay or cushioning under a more decorative fabric, now makes a serious fashion statement. Plastic used to be seen as horrible, tacky and cheap, but now it's the last word in urban chic. Concrete was strictly functional and best kept hidden until minimalists rediscovered its potential. Brightly coloured laminated worktops are now back in demand.

ABOVE **The way to use texture in a neutral palette is to set different weaves, stripes or smooth surfaces against each other. Here we have a corded carpet on the horizontal, with woven baskets on the diagonal to create an energetic textural contrast. The papier-mâché bowl breaks up the pattern and the even smoother stick adds a tactile finishing touch.**

CREATING INTEREST

Texture does not only replace colour – it can also be used exclusively for its tactile and visual qualities. The roughness, smoothness or spikiness of a surface describes its texture. There are endless variations and combinations of textures that can be brought into play to make the home environment a more interesting and stimulating place.

Houses are being built faster than ever these days, with less attention to detail, and wherever we live most of us do it in an arrangement of smooth-sided, interconnecting box shapes. Old houses are more likely to have interesting architectural features to break up the monotony of plain walls, such as plaster mouldings, high skirting boards, and dado and picture rails. In their absence, there are many wall coverings and specialist paints that can be used to add interest. Anaglypta is a wall texture that has been around for more than a hundred years. The raised patterns were often used in heavy-duty areas such as hallways and staircases, where they adhered with such ferocity that any attempt to remove them brought most of the plaster off the wall as well. The original company still produces textured wall coverings, and has new ranges that look perfect in contemporary rooms. A more recent arrival is a wallpaper range with a raised texture in metallic finishes, which mimics aluminium flooring. It makes the full industrial look much more accessible and less of a permanent commitment, as the surfaces can be painted over with ordinary emulsion paint. Other new textures in wallpaper are a mixture of rough and smooth geometric patterns, widely spaced medallion shapes and ranges of natural materials such as bamboo, linen or woven reed panels. Cork is another warm, interesting natural texture due for a comeback – it looks good with dark wood, leather and chrome furniture in sculptural modern shapes, and as a bonus it provides excellent noise insulation.

One of the reasons that the colours we choose from a paint chart surprise us by looking different on our walls is that any variation in texture will introduce elements of light and shade to alter the regularity of the colour. Clever use of texture can really add depth to a colour scheme, making the difference between an ordinary and an exceptional room.

Our eyes are constantly travelling over surfaces and colours to evaluate and balance what we see. Clever interior designers understand this, and provide interest and relaxation in equal measures, making a room as visually satisfying and comfortable as possible.

ABOVE **This bathroom has an enamelled iron bath with bright chrome taps and wood panelling on the walls. The starfish, shells, sponges and pebbles effectively recreate a sense of the shoreline.**

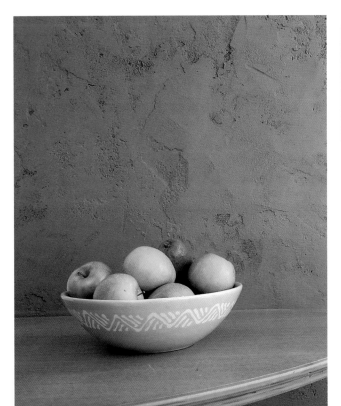

FAMILIAR TEXTURES

Some of the instantly familiar textures used in the home include: leather • suède • linen • cotton • wool • rattan • paper • rubber • corrugated cardboard • silk • velvet • wood • slate • glass • stone • shell • glazed and unglazed ceramics • cork • marble • PVC • fleece • fake fur • hard plastic • stainless steel • wire mesh • concrete • chrome • rough and smooth wood • foam • feathers • bamboo

LEFT **Green-grey walls with an extreme rustic finish have the potential to look dark and gloomy, but the juxtapostion of a fine wooden table gives a stunningly sophisticated effect. The lilac-glazed ceramic bowl and the high shine of the green apples add two more textures to this very intriguing environment.**

Paint effects

 Paint effects have come a long way in recent years – not only do contemporary paint effects look better, but successful application is also a lot easier to achieve. The big paint companies have all produced ranges of special effect products, which are easy to use and guarantee good results. There is a textured paint to make new walls look like those of an old farmhouse. There are shiny, metallic paints that simulate hard metal, and there are even textile finishes to make your walls look like faded denim jeans.

EASY EFFECTS

Paint effects are fun, and there are several that require no specialist training.

WOODGRAINING AND DRAGGING

Essentially woodgraining and dragging are the same kinds of effect; they are both created by dragging a dry paintbrush through an oil-based glaze in the direction of the woodgrain. The difference is that in woodgraining you can create effects beyond that of imitating the pattern of the grain.

STENCILLING AND SPONGING

It comes as no surprise that stencilling is staging a comeback, because it is the easiest and least expensive way of applying a pattern. Everyone can cut a simple stencil, and there are thousands of more complex designs on the market. Stencilling is something most of us tackle as children but feel wary of trying on the walls. The first secret of stencilling success is using a removable spray adhesive on the back of the stencil so that it sticks to the wall as you paint. The second one is

ABOVE, LEFT **Woodgraining: you can use a graining comb to make attractive patterns by dragging the comb through an oil-based glaze.**

LEFT **A denim effect wall finish is a soft blue finish available in kit form. The wall is first coated in a pale blue, then rollered over in a denim blue glaze, which is dragged with a long-haired brush.**

RIGHT **Stencil cutting is easier if you stick the pattern onto the card or plastic with a removable spray. Use a very sharp craft knife, inserting the point and cutting away from any corners. Protect the work surface with a cutting mat or cardboard.**

BELOW **Sponging can be done with a natural sponge and paint should be applied quite sparingly. Here a contrasting colour is used to demonstrate the technique and a subtler effect can be achieved with a softer combination of colours. Rotate the sponge as you work to avoid a repetitious pattern.**

to dip your brush in the paint then wipe it on kitchen paper to remove all the moist paint and just leave a dry coating of colour. You can always apply more colour, but too much will cause blobbing and runs. The same rule applies to sponging, when paint should be applied with a light touch. The textured finishes are applied as a thick coating of plaster-based paint, which is then worked on with a brush, comb or sponge to score into the surface and lift some of the coating.

ABOVE **Use a comb or piece of plastic cut to size to create a pattern. This can simply be directional or geometric as here, with one square vertical one horizontal, or you could design your own effect.**

RIGHT **A sponge dabbed onto a textured base will create a simple raised pattern. This can look good in a rustic-style room, and can also be re-painted with a foam roller.**

FAR RIGHT **Roll a set of vertical stripes onto the wall from bottom to top and then paint a set of horizontal stripes in another colour with a roller to create this check effect.**

Shades of white

COLOUR PALETTE

White comes in a great many subtle variations of colour and tone. Just one white standing alone is easily described. It is simply – white. A selection of whites seen together reveal that tones of white can be warm, cool, dull, bright, old, faded, blue, brown and many more possibilities besides. Brilliant white is the most reflective of all of the whites, and can be hard and dazzling when compared with a colour such as bone white, which is warm, soft and natural, or blue white, which is fresh and cool.

The many white variations that we can now buy as named paint colours have been created to meet the demand for colour-free decorating schemes based on the idea of a 'pure' style. Colour and synthetics have no place in this white world, only natural fabrics and materials in a variety of white textures used together to create a harmonious, peaceful environment. The only acceptable colour here is the natural wood used for furniture and flooring, or the living green leaves of an indoor plant. It may sound like an impossible dream, but if the style is used in just one room it is simplicity itself. A bedroom or bathroom will be easiest, but good storage is essential because colourful clutter will ruin the effect.

Bedroom sanctuary

Use a chalky white distemper paint for the walls. Floors can be sanded and polished if the wood is pale, otherwise floorboards can be painted white. Scattered sheepskins or white flokati rugs are the perfect way to create islands of warmth on wooden floors, and make the most deliciously soft bedside rugs. Sheer, floaty white curtain panels, white

wooden shutters or natural linen blinds are all suitable for windows – much depends upon the aspect and the shape of your windows. Almost any style of furniture, old or new, can be used, so long as all fabrics are natural. An ordinary bed can be transformed into a four-poster by building a simple wooden frame surround and draping it with white muslin tab-topped curtains.

Bathroom sanctuary

This could be achieved with the most basic DIY toolkit and skills.

If your bathroom suite is white then you are already halfway there, and white-painted wood panelling or white tiles and towels are all you need. Textural contrasts will make the room look more interesting – matt for woodwork, gleaming tiles, polished chrome and folded fluffy towels. Flooring could be a good white marble-effect vinyl, or pale grey and white checks with white cotton-twist rugs. Frosted windows with a slight green tint will add extra freshness to a bathroom, and a pretty voile curtain panel will add a softening touch. If any colour is used, stick to the very palest shades of grey, fawn or aqua.

PROJECT
White-on-white stencil effect

YOU WILL NEED:

Two shades of white
paint with contrasting
finishes (such as satin
and chalky finish)

Stencil material

A photocopy of
the pattern

Spraymount

Craft knife

Broad stencil brush

Cloth

Plumb line (optional)

Spirit level (optional)

1

2

3

The idea is to stencil a pattern of
contrasting textures, which can either be
rough/smooth, chalky/glossy or matt/glitter.
The pattern is based on a geometric shape
that is easy to enlarge and cut out. It can
be stencilled in a regular grid pattern, or
used randomly for a more casual effect.

A compromise between the two is best for
large areas, moving a plumb line along a wall
at regular intervals as a guide and stencilling
in a half-drop pattern. Decide on the distance
between the motifs, and stagger the rows so
that in each alternate row the first motif falls
halfway between those in the row before.

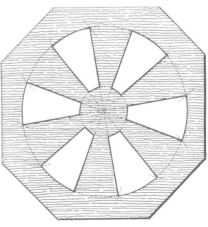

COLOUR KEY

1 Creamy white

2 Off-white

3 Peach white

TEMPLATE

This pattern can either be
constructed using a compass and
a ruler or, simpler still, make
a photocopied enlargement of this
diagram to the size of your choice.

HOW TO DO IT

Stencilling a grid of bold shapes on the wall is simple and will give a very contemporary look to any room. To divide a wall into a grid use a plumb line to mark the verticals and a ruler with a spirit level for the horizontals.

STEP 1 Enlarge the pattern and apply a light drift of Spraymount to the back. Stick it onto a sheet of stencil card or mylar (the clear plastic stencil material).

STEP 2 Cut out the pattern with a craft knife, always cutting away from the corners towards the middle.

STEP 3 Paint the wall with the matt white paint and leave till bone dry.

STEP 4 Spray the back of the stencil with Spraymount and set aside. It should dry to a tacky finish that will stick to the wall when you are stencilling but be easily removed without leaving any sticky residue.

STEP 5 Place the stencil on the wall and use the chalky paint undiluted, applying a generous coating through the stencil with a broad stencil brush.

STEP 6 Lift the stencil and wipe the edges before repositioning it.

Neutrals

The term 'neutral' applies to a range of indistinct tones and shades derived from mixtures of black and white with brown, grey, or sometimes with lesser amounts of muddy green, yellow or blue. A neutral colour scheme might be based around soft blue-toned grey or pale khaki brown, but whatever the slight colour cast, there will always be a high proportion of white. The neutrals are usually taken from the colour of a natural material such as parchment, sand, stone or marble, and work well with natural textures and materials.

A neutral colour scheme does not have to omit colour altogether, but the proportion of any other colours used should be small enough so as not to override its basic neutrality. Pattern is one way that a colour can be used without overpowering a scheme intended to be seen as neutral. This will work particularly well if the pattern combines the predominant neutral and a colour.

A colour scheme based around a single neutral does not have to look monotonous if an interesting mixture of tones and textures is used.

Sophisticated beige

A mid-beige vinyl silk paint on walls, with a dead flat darker mushroom beige on all woodwork and an almost white ceiling, does not sound all that thrilling. But add rough woven matting flooring, a large brown and white cowhide rug, loose-weave drapes and a slatted wooden blind, a pale linen-covered sofa with dark beige suede cushions and a mohair throw, and the room has become the epitome of contemporary sophistication. The same theory can be applied to any neutral decorating scheme.

Tranquil haven

A neutral colour scheme is superbly restful on the eyes. If you spend your days in an industrial environment or in the heart of a busy city, then this sort of room will be a haven of tranquillity at the end of the day. If a room is mainly used in the daytime, a pale neutral scheme will make the most of any natural light, which can be filtered using sheer muslin panels over the windows.

If a room is inclined to feel cold, make your selection from the warmer neutrals with yellowish tones, like cream, sand and pale straw. They look very good with pale greys or grey-greens. The cooler stone greys can be warmed up by the inclusion of a pinky beige.

Neutral backgrounds may be safe, but they certainly don't have to be dull or boring. A room painted in tones of stone grey on walls, ceiling and floor is like a vessel waiting to be filled. Strong colour statements can be saved for soft furnishings, contemporary furniture, paintings and dramatic lighting, even flower arrangements. Imagine the grey room with purple floor length curtains, leather and chrome classic chairs, a red sofa, a row of coloured neon tubes and a giant cactus plant.

PROJECT
Calico drapes

YOU WILL NEED:

Unbleached calico, wide enough for two curtains to cover the window – measure from floor to ceiling and multiply by four (this is to allow for a generous draped heading and some billowing of the curtains onto the floor)

Staple gun and staples

Iron-on bonding tape or double-sided tape for hems

Step ladder

Tie-back hooks

This is a project for those who enjoy a touch of drama with their decorating. It requires no sewing; it can be managed without a pin or a pair of scissors – but you'll need another pair of hands and a stepladder.

It is an unconventional but effective and economical way to drape a large window. The idea is simple enough – to use a single, long length of unbleached calico as two curtains and a draped heading, which is attached to the window frame using a staple gun.

If there is no wooden window frame, a batten fixed above the window would serve the same purpose.

TEMPLATE

Divide the length of fabric in half and mark the centre line (above). Measure the window width; transfer the measurement to the fabric, the centre line running down the middle. Hold the length of fabric up to the batten and staple the two corners of the first marked line to the batten (above). Pleat (see opposite).

With one side pleated and stapled, pick up the length at the second marked line on the far edge and staple it up to the end of the batten (above, right). Staple the near edge to meet the first drop. Curtains are tied back during the day.

COLOUR KEY
1 Dusky blue
2 Maize
3 Hemp
4 Warm grey

HOW TO DO IT

This is such a stunning window treatment and much easier to do than to explain! It's like riding a bicycle – once learned never forgotten.

STEP 1 Hem one raw edge, and with a generous amount of this end resting on the floor on the left side of the window, take the rest of the fabric up the ladder with you. Line the fabric up with the top of the window frame and fold it over, allowing the excess to drop. Staple the fabric to the frame to overlap the centre of the window frame by 25mm/1in, then staple the other side to the window frame on the left. Much will depend on the type of window frame, but aim to conceal the top of the frame under the fabric.

STEP 2 If the fabric's width is much greater than half the window, then you will need to pleat the curtain. To do this, find the middle and staple it to the middle of the frame. Do the same again on each side of it, and then again, until all the slack is taken up in evenly stapled pleats. Now move the ladder to the other side of the window.

STEP 3 Drape the length of fabric across the top of the window until you reach the right edge of the frame. The line between the corners should fall in a gentle curve (see diagram). Now twist the fabric over, taking the right edge under the drape and into the centre, so that the rest of it falls to make the second curtain. Staple this right side curtain, pleating across the top in the same way as the left side.

STEP 4 Finish off the draped heading by gathering up and stapling the fabric in the middle, so that it falls in even drapes. Make sure that all the staples are concealed by the folds of fabric. Finally, fix tieback hooks into the sides of the window frame so that the curtains can be gathered up and tied back during the day.

COLOUR
PALETTE

3-D effects with colour

Colour can make a wall shimmer, fade, dazzle or confuse. The most obvious 3-D effect is produced by using a light/dark contrast to create a drop shadow. This can create illusions such as simple raised panels, recessed niches or intricate plaster mouldings. Coloured shapes can be shaded to give them form and the shape of a room can be dramatically changed by the introduction of a false sense of perspective. Once you understand the advancing and receding qualities of different colours you can produce very convincing effects.

The Ndbele tribeswomen in South Africa paint their simple mud huts externally with architectural features such as columns, pediments, archways and castellated walls. The background is whitewash, with black outlines and patterns filled in with brilliant colours. It is an idea that can be seen in many parts of the world where paint is used in bold and creative ways to imitate ornate architecture. In Mexico, houses are painted vivid colours with striped bands of contrasting colours. Wall paintings often create 3-D effects and murals are an important part of the local culture.

Trompe l'œil

Expert trompe l'œil painters create convincing illusions such as
- walls of shelves stacked with books
- doorways where they don't exist
- windows looking out on panoramic views

and many other special effects. Some painters even go so far as to create whole room sets and pastoral scenes on living room and bedroom walls, complete with painted furniture, drawers spilling open to show beautifully painted fabric folds.

There is no need to be that ambitious (unless of course you have the artistic ability!) but there is a lot of fun to be had by using 3-D effects to add life and interest to a featureless room.

In a very plain and box-shaped room, a painted frieze of light and dark geometric shapes can be drawn out with templates. If the angles and the direction of the light are plotted correctly, the effect will be simply stunning and will add a new lease of life to what was previously quite a dull room.

The 3-D project included in this section shows you how to paint blocks of colour with dropped shadows. This is a very basic 3-D effect that can be used in a striking way or in a very toned-down way, depending on which room in the house you choose to use it.

It can be a popular choice in living rooms, but it may be best to use small blocks of subtle colours – large blocks of primary colours may prove difficult to live with.

This is a good look in a modern decorating scheme with the minimum of clutter, so there is nothing to take the eye away from the impact of the colour blocks.

Go on, dive into the world of 3-D!

PROJECT
Blocks of colour with dropped shadow

COLOUR
PALETTE

YOU WILL NEED:

Long rule with a
spirit level

Pencil or chalk

Plumb line

Set square

Decorator's
masking tape

Colour for blocks

Shadow colour

Small roller and tray

Paintbrush
(25mm/1in)

This is the simplest three-dimensional effect, whose impact increases with the size of the shapes. The colours chosen for the blocks can be as subtle or bold as you choose. If the room style is based around neutral colours, then using two tones of stone grey will create a subtle panelled effect. On the other hand, primary colours with black shadows on a white background will make the blocks of colour appear to leap off the wall. Much depends upon the room's shape, size and purpose. But beware – a bedazzling optical effect would soon become tiresome in an everyday living room.

COLOUR KEY

1 Avocado

2 Red salmon

3 Pure blue

4 Black

HOW TO DO IT

Treat your wall as a blank canvas and create this dramatic effect in the boldest of colours. A 45° set square and a ruler with a straight edge are the essential tools for the job.

STEP 1 Measure the area and calculate the size and positions of the colour blocks. Drop the plumb line to use as a vertical guide and use the long rule to mark out rectangular shapes in pencil.

STEP 2 Place a strip of masking tape around each of the shapes then apply the colour with the small roller. Leave to dry, then peel off the tape. Leave overnight until bone dry.

STEP 3 Use the set square to draw a shadow box at 45° on one side and the base of each block. Place a strip of masking tape around the shadow area, including the two inside edges of the colour block.

STEP 4 Paint the shadow with the brush and leave the paint to dry before peeling off the tape.

Colour Highlights

Attracting attention and maybe distracting the eye from a less deserving area is the general idea of a highlight, and colour can be used very effectively in this capacity. Colour highlights can also create a more energetic environment, but in order to work they have to be seen against a neutral or tonally similar background – they are no good if the room is already a total riot of colour! The secret of colour highlighting is that the strongest impact is achieved when the highlight colour is used in moderation – too much and it becomes a feature, too little and it can become overlooked. Remember that the highlight does not have to be a strongly saturated colour – a flash of pale apricot seen against dark grey would be as effective as violet purple against baby pink.

Adding focus

The process of decorating involves a lot of visualisation, preparation, shopping and plain hard work. The inspiration for a colour scheme or room style may have come from something seen in a magazine, on holiday or in someone else's home, but the results are disappointing because, although the general look is the same, something is missing. The room has changed, but with all the hard work completed an extra something is needed to pull the look together. This something is the room's focus.

THE CREATIVE PATH

Most rooms will have some individuality, a feature such as the fireplace, a doorway, a nice floor or perhaps a style of window that becomes the natural focal point. If nothing is striking enough to become an area of focus, then one can be created with colour. This could be done with paint; it could be as simple as painting a contrasting coloured shape on one of the walls, or painting blocks of colour as broad borders for framed pictures. More often, though, it is done by introducing some new element, which could be a painting, a sculptural piece of furniture, a rug or a wonderful plant. This does not necessarily mean spending a lot of money. The art could be a row of pebbles in a straight line; a strangely shaped piece of driftwood displayed on a bright background, or a pile of pine cones sprayed shocking pink. A canvas floorcloth can be painted and stencilled for a fraction of the cost of buying a rug, or you could paint a rug directly onto the floor. It is important to enjoy the decorating process, and taking the creative route is always more rewarding than shopping – well, nearly always!

LEFT **This circular rug has radiating coloured lines that attract the eye to its colour, shape and size. A bare floor is fine for dancing, but rugs make a room much more homely.**

KEEPING THINGS IN PROPORTION

Proportion is very important, as there is a big difference between attracting attention and dominating a room. An exuberant palm in a ceramic pot looks great – as long as it's not so great as to infringe on your space! In just the same way, something that is far too small in proportion to its surroundings doesn't work either. A small handmade designer rug will still attract attention in the middle of a large open expanse of floor, but it will look mean.

SMART BUT SIMPLE

Choosing wisely does not always mean spending a lot of money. One idea which works very well is repetition. Instead of buying one large vase, buy four in the same style but in different colours, and arrange them in a straight line. This will create a colour rhythm and focus, and need not cost very much at all. The same could be done with something completely free, like green-tinged

cola bottles, which are design classics. A line of them becomes a sculpture in the right setting.

Fresh flowers are the most reliable way of adding instant focus to a room. Depending on what you choose, flowers can be used to change the mood of the room – they can even be used to reflect your own mood, if you like! For instance, if you're feeling romantic, choose roses; and if you're feeling full of the joys of life and you don't care who knows it, go for lilies. Many flowers come in a whole range of gorgeous colours, so you should have no problem working with your room's colour scheme, and changing the atmosphere throughout the year. An arrangement of striking seedheads from the garden can also make a really stunning display.

If a bunch of flowers seems too much of an indulgence, just buy one or two single stems and angle a spotlight their way. This little trick creates a tremendously cool, contemporary effect.

Window treatments

 Windows are one of the main focal points in any room because of the light coming in and the view of the outside world that they reveal. Windows also give us an opportunity to introduce colour and pattern that will flatter the room's colour scheme and pick up on colours used elsewhere in the room. The biggest mistake is to treat the window in isolation without taking the rest of the room into account, because the right window treatment will make any room look a hundred times better.

ABOVE **When a room has a fabulous view, nothing should be allowed to interfere or detract from it. Window frame colours or curtains should create a perfect frame for the view, choosing either a strong contrast as an outline or a harmonious shade to create a more natural progression from room to view. In this room there are no curtains to complicate the scene, and the frames have been painted to match the blue-green of the trees.**

THE RIGHT TREATMENT

There are so many different ways of covering windows, and some solutions will only suit certain situations. Consider whether the room is mainly to be used during the day or at night, what the room's purpose is, and if there are any practical limitations on the type of window treatment that would suit the room. In a room which has direct early morning sunlight, curtains will need black-out linings or blinds; one that is overlooked by other windows will need muslins or nets for privacy, and windows opening onto a busy street will soon make curtains grimy and the chosen fabric will need to be one that will not deteriorate with regular washing.

Sometimes, the view from a window is simply too stunning to conceal – a view of city lights at night, for instance, can be hundred times better than the same view during the day when it would be better obscured by slatted blinds, which would also soften and filter the light. A large picture-window view over a garden or fields will be the room's best feature in daylight, but can make the inhabitants feel too exposed after dark, when thick drapes would make the room feel more intimate. Ruling out specific window treatments is helpful as this will help to narrow down the options and allow you to focus on what will look best.

When in doubt, do something creative and temporary while you decide. If there is a curtain rail, use cotton sheets or saris, draped or with curtain clips.

SUBTLE CO-ORDINATION

The over-co-ordinated decorating style where the same fabric is used for furnishings and curtains is very dated, and looks as impersonal as a hotel or a furniture showroom. Try picking up a theme instead with, for instance, sari-style fabric used for curtains and embroidered silk cushions in matching colours, making a link between the furniture and the window treatment. A crocheted white lace panel pinned across a window in a simple Mediterranean-style bedroom will echo the lace cloth on a bedside table. A bright orange roller blind will warm up a shaded north-facing window, and something as simple as a bowl of oranges will match the colour and balance its brilliance in the room.

ABOVE **Simple roller blinds are one of the most economical window treatments and they have the added benefit of obscuring only a small part of the window surface. This means they can be adjusted to allow maximum light into a room when needed or pulled down to reveal the pattern and provide privacy in the evening.**

LEFT **It would be a pity to hide a deep window recess like the one in this cottage. The wooden panelling adds to the sense of perspective and creates the perfect frame for the flower arrangement. Painting a deep recess in light gloss paint will bring more light into the room.**

Window treatments

CURTAINS AND BLINDS

If walls are painted in plain colours then curtains can be patterned in harmonious or contrasting colours, but when using pattern proportion is very important. As a rule, large patterns need large areas and small patterns work best when they are seen at close range.

Coloured transparent fabrics look pale with daylight shining through them, but their colour looks stronger in the evening, especially if the windows are fitted with roller blinds. Blinds are a good way of adding colour to a room, and a contemporary-styled room with a row of windows looks good with a different colour blind in each one. A blind fitted into the window recess can remain in place if curtains are added, but will also look good on its own.

Roman blinds are very easy to make – they hang in folds, and can be made in most fabric weights from heavy canvas to soft voile. They are also the most economical treatment as they hang as a flat panel to match the dimensions of the window.

When in doubt, choose a plain neutral colour and a classic window treatment rather than something wildly fashionable if you are buying a good quality fabric, as this will not date. If you are on a tight budget, investigate alternative fabrics, especially from street markets near garment-making districts, e.g., unbleached calico, bed sheeting, felt, fleece or suit linings.

LEFT This light, harmonious and thoroughly grown-up living room has been designed around a single shade of lilac. The furniture, woodwork and soft furnishings all match, and the gingham and plaid check of the curtains prevents the effect from becoming too bland.

ABOVE Full-length yellow curtains frame this window, and the sun filters through to cast a warm glow of light into the room. The soft furnishing colours used here are cool, with greens and blues mellowed by the brilliance of the yellow curtains. When drawn, the curtains almost fill the wall, making an even bolder yellow statement.

LEFT Floral Roman blinds with a dark border are teamed with simple sprigged muslin curtains for these glazed doors. This is a perfect solution for doors that are often in use, as they can be left open to admit the light or closed to provide shade.

Soft furnishings

Soft furnishings are the fabrics we use in the home to add character and instil our own personalities. As very few of us undertake the making or even re-upholstery of sofas, armchairs or beds, it's the cushions, shawls, throws, lampshades, tablecloths and bedspreads we add that change something mass-produced into something uniquely ours. The idea is make the room look more attractive and increase the level of comfort, so choose soft fillings and fabrics that are tactile as well as beautiful.

ABOVE **Choose cushions of the same style in different colours to give a harmonious look. These embroidered cushions in purple and olive are exotic and inviting against deep rose chenille upholstery.**

RING THE CHANGES

Soft furnishings can be changed with the seasons, creating a light, airy style in summer and a warm comfort zone for the winter. A sofa can be covered with a fleece throw for winter and cotton for summer. In the days before central heating, this was a normal part of home life, with soft flannel sheets and woolly rugs for winter and crisp cotton sheets and light woven floor mats in summer. Winter curtains were heavy and thick to block out the cold draughts, but summer was a time for net, lace and cheerful cotton prints. Nostalgia can be fun and there is always room for retro style in fashion.

Colour has a huge role to play in soft furnishings, especially if the room is simply decorated in plain colours. A room could be painted off-white with unbleached muslin curtains and chair covers, but still be perceived as colourful if the sofa and chairs were piled with an assortment of vividly coloured cushions, the floor boasted a bright patterned dhurrie and the table lamps had equally vibrant shades. To see how soft furnishings can alter a room's character, first imagine a golden yellow bedroom with an iron bed draped with a rich red velvet bedspread and bolster cushions, then change the bedding to a blue and white striped duvet cover. The whole mood has swung from luxurious and exotic to fresh and breezy. Put the idea into practice by using different fabrics and accessories in your bedroom to spice it up or cool it down to suit the mood.

COLOUR CO-ORDINATION

A monochrome colour scheme can look bland without the right type of soft furnishings. One solution is to choose a range of patterned fabrics that are not usually seen together, in a single colour. This could mean mixing classic patterns such as toile de jouy, stripes, tie-dye circles and floral damask to make a set of unmatched cushions. Keep the rest of the room neutral and leave the cushions to make the colour statement. The beauty of this style of colour co-ordinating is that you can usually buy remnants of expensive fabric in amounts sufficient for cushion covers at a fraction of the cost of buying it off the roll. Make it a rule always to have a rummage in remnant bins anyway, and build up a treasure chest of fabric for future soft furnishing projects.

LEFT **Rich, varied textures and weights of fabrics in shades of yellow.**

ABOVE **The secret of creating a Japanese look means taking a no-frills, minimalist approach to both colour and design. Cream, red and black are all the colours you need.**

LEFT **A thick gold and red curtain softens the hard edges of the doorway, and the same colours are picked up in the soft covers of the dining chairs in the background. A band of contrasting colour could be used to join short remnants of superior quality fabrics and create a luxurious draped curtain like this one at a bargain price.**

Painted floors

The idea of painting floors is a very old one that has become popular once again. One of the most attractive aspects of floor painting is how inexpensive it is in comparison to other floor treatments. A floor often needs only a light sanding to prepare it and many paint companies have added special floor paints to their product ranges. If you use conventional paint, add a couple of coats of strong polyurethane varnish to keep the colour fresh or, for a more lived-in style, just let the wear and tear show through.

PREPARING THE FLOOR

If you are thinking of painting the floor and have first to dispose of carpets or old vinyl, it is wise to have a peep underneath to assess the condition of the floorboards. If the flooring has been stuck to the boards with carpet tape you will need to use a sander to remove the sticky tape. If the floor would benefit from a good sanding then it would be best to hire a machine for a day. The sanding machine hire is not hugely expensive but cost of the special sandpaper can add up, so do make it clear in the rental shop that you are sanding to prepare for painting rather than to expose the true beauty of the natural wood. Using a sanding machine does not require great effort but it creates a lot of noise and dust and you have first to remove everything from its path. Once the floor has been sanded it can be wiped over with sugar soap and left to dry before painting.

The most important thing to remember when painting a floor is to begin in the far corner and end in the doorway! A standard paint roller and tray do the job very well unless you are painting the boards different colours, when it is advisable to use a small foam roller or a paintbrush. The paint is best applied in thin coats with adequate drying time between.

Patterned floors can either be stencilled or marked out in chalk and filled in with a paintbrush. One of the most timeless painted patterns is a simple chequerboard which can be painted directly onto floorboards or onto sheets of hardboard tacked over the boards if you prefer a smoother 'marble' finish.

There are several ways of painting a chequerboard, which can be done diagonally or horizontally. Masking tape can be used to outline the squares. It makes painting easier, but mask and paint only a few squares at a time because it can cause confusion and ruin the pattern over a large area. The simplest method is to mark out the floor in pencil or chalk by drawing round a square template. The stark contrast of black and white can be very unforgiving of any wobbly edges, so choose grey, coffee brown or sage green and off-white instead for a softer but very stylish flooring effect.

SPECIAL FLOOR PAINTS

You can now buy paint made specially for vinyl floors, which means an end to the days of putting up with nasty patterns when you move into a new place, just because the flooring is in too good a condition to justify replacing it. All you need is a pot of paint and a roller to transform a bad floor with a tasteful matt dusky blue, sandy yellow or barn red. Now that's progress!

There are also specialist paints for concrete floors that give a more finished, homely look. Concrete is a cold indoor flooring material suitable only for warm climates or conservatories. It is popular in the South of France, where stunning patterned floors are created with inlays of beach pebbles.

PROJECT
Painting a floor

Once you have decided to paint a floor, everything will have to be removed from the floor area. Examine the floorboards closely, checking for any protruding nails, which should be banged in using a hammer with a nail punch. Splintered boards must be sanded and any holes filled with a good quality wood filler. Sand the floor lightly, then sweep up all the dust and wash the boards with a sugar soap solution to get rid of any grease. A proper floor paint will give the best finish and last the longest; otherwise, apply two coats of floor quality varnish after the paint.

HOW TO DO IT

Painting a floor in a single colour could not be simpler. It does not take long and the effect will be one of instant freshness.

STEP 1 Mask off the skirting boards to floor level.

STEP 2 Begin with the brush, painting the primer into the edges of the floor, right into the corners and up to the masking tape.

STEP 3 Then apply the primer to the rest of the boards with the roller, and leave to dry. Apply the floor paint in exactly the same way. Two thin coats will give a better finish than one thick one.

STEP 4 Leave the paint to dry overnight for the best results. Carefully remove the masking tape from the skirting boards.

Creating a Style
With Colour

Certain colour combinations have become synonymous with particular places – this is due to the rich variety of historical and cultural influences in our world, as well as the differences between urban or rural environments and hot or cool climates. Colours can also evoke very strong memories and associations, and these transport us to faraway places. A holiday postcard can become the basis for a whole new decorating scheme, with chalky white paint and bright blue woodwork reflecting the Greek islands, for example, or faded earthy colours bringing back the essence of elegant Venice. The most important thing when you are planning on recreating the style of anywhere, however, is to get the colours exactly right.

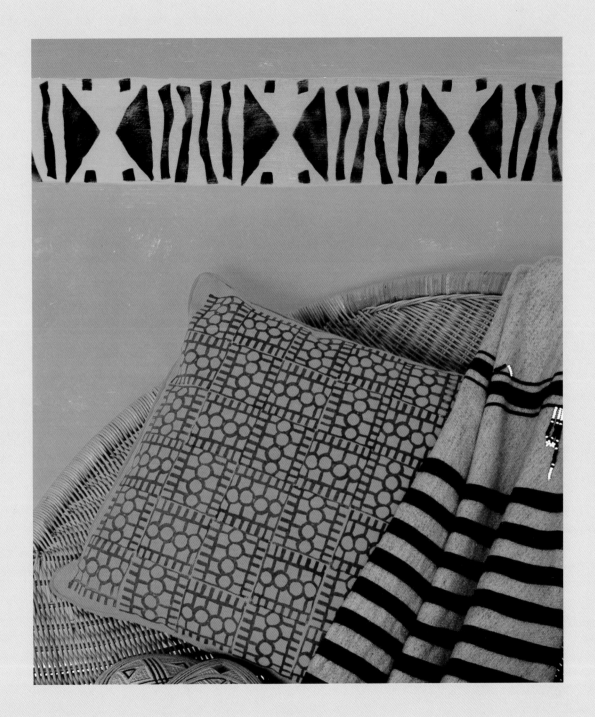

English country

The English country cottage is a very cosy and welcoming place where there are roses and honeysuckle around the door in summer and usually a freshly baked cake for tea. In the winter time there will always be a log fire burning in the grate and a soft wool shawl draped over the back of the sofa for that little bit of extra warmth. If you get the look right, visitors should immediately feel so at home that they flop down in a comfortable chair, put their feet up and ask for a cup of tea. In fact, you may have to use force to evict them!

English country style is eclectic, and only really works well when old and new are mixed together. Aim for the impression that furniture and accessories have been passed down through the family for several generations. If you are starting from scratch, shop around at antique markets, boot sales and craft fairs. The right framed mirror or china bowl can make all the difference and need not cost a fortune – imperfections, chips and worn edges actually enhance the look.

Pattern is one of the key ingredients, and many different styles can be successfully combined, including woven woollen plaids, Indian and Turkish rugs, tapestries, plain and floral cotton chintz, damask and lace.

Old and mellow

Floral patterned fabrics are now produced in soft faded colours, or you could search out genuine vintage fabrics at jumble sales or flea markets. One old chintz curtain can make a whole set of plump cushions if you're handy with a sewing machine.

In old country cottages with exposed beams, walls are usually rough plaster painted white, pink or creamy yellow. Low ceilings and small windows can make rooms dark and gloomy, but by painting window recesses glossy white you can virtually double the amount of incoming natural light. Another trick is to position mirrors opposite windows to reflect the light back into the room.

Faking it

If you don't have a sweet little beamed country cottage, but still want to decorate in the English Country style, the first thing to consider is the proportions of the room. Even the most boxy plain room can be made to look a lot cosier with the right wall treatment, colours and lighting. Walls can be tongue and groove panelled up to picture rail height with a shelf running above the panelling. Or apply a rough textured paint to give the impression of an uneven surface and rough plasterwork. Stencilling works well on rough surfaces and is perfect in a country setting. Patterns can either be cut at home, taking inspiration from textiles in the room, or bought ready-cut.

The key colours are taken straight from the cottage garden: soft powder blue, cream, all shades of pink, pale, moss and grass green, brown and brick red.

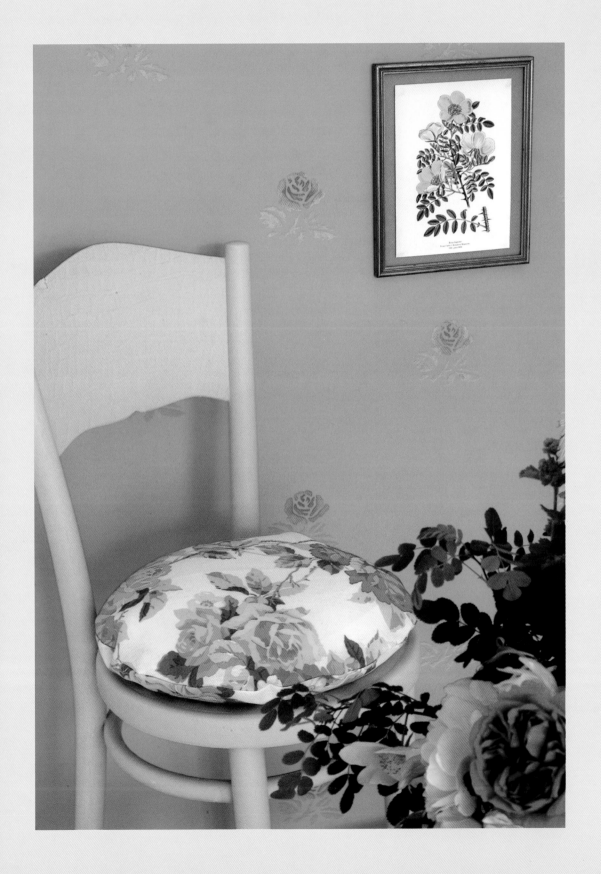

PROJECT
A rose-stencilled wall

YOU WILL NEED:

Powder blue paint for
background

Sample pots of
two pinks

Sample pot of green

Stencil material
(mylar or stencil card
if you prefer), or buy a
ready-cut rose stencil

Spraymount

Scalpel or craft knife

3 stencil brushes

3 white saucers

Plumb line

Square of card (to
mark distance
between motifs)

If you like pattern and have uneven walls, then stencilling is the way to go, as wallpaper requires walls that are smooth and even. This is a very romantic, feminine style for a pretty bedroom. The blue rose-patterned walls have a look of faded textiles and combine well with lace, muslin and plenty of vintage floral fabrics used for cushions and bed covers. The walls provide a perfect backdrop for traditional bedroom furniture like dressing tables, Lloyd loom chairs, iron bedsteads and wardrobes. Keep a look-out for pretty old vases, mirrors and lamps that will add authenticity to the look.

COLOUR KEY

1 Soft peacock blue

2 Deep rose pink

3 Pale pistachio

4 Rose pink

TEMPLATE

Copy this pattern or enlarge it using the grid system. We used the rose pattern at the size of 60mm/2½in across. The stencil can be cut from waxed card or special stencil plastic available from craft stores.

HOW TO DO IT

Stencilling a wall pattern is quicker than putting up wallpaper and also a lot cheaper. Use the smallest amount of paint on your brush and practise on paper before you tackle the wall.

STEP 1 Make the pattern for the stencil. Coat the back of the pattern with Spraymount and stick it onto the stencil material. Use a sharp craft knife and cut out the stencil carefully.

STEP 2 Peel off the paper pattern, then spray the back of the stencil with Spraymount and leave it to become tacky.

STEP 3 Hang the plumb line 250mm/10in from one corner of the wall and position the card with the line running through two corners. Make a pencil mark at each corner, then move the card down, placing the top point on the lowest mark, and repeat to skirting. Mark up the whole wall in this way.

STEP 4 Position the stencil and smooth it onto the wall. Put the paints on the saucers and dab off brushes with kitchen paper so little remains on the brush.

STEP 5 Begin stencilling with the dark pink in the middle of the rose, then move on to the pale pink for the outer petals. Lift the stencil to check on the result as you go.

STEP 6 Use the green paint for the leaves and stem. Lift the stencil to check the result. Position it on the next mark and repeat the pattern until the wall is covered with roses.

Pure Romany

COLOUR
PALETTE

Romany style is most suited to people who prefer to keep one foot in the past and whose idea of bliss is a country kitchen with a cooking range. Rich, dark background colours are decorated using the light touch of single free-hand brushstrokes, with each pattern being composed of a mixture of stripes, swirls, dots and curves. Romany inspiration comes from the countryside and nature; flowers are the most popular decorative motif. Red, green, black and white are the main colours, but many other colours can be used for the decoration.

The colours explode with all the fun of the fair. Bright canal barges, decks piled high with vividly patterned tinware, fairground stalls and painted gypsy caravans are the inspiration for this look. Painting patterns were handed down through Romany families, and as lifestyles changed many of the traditional skills have disappeared. Fortunately the lazy, slow, canal-boat lifestyle appealed to people looking for an escape route from the fast pace of modern life, and since the Seventies many canal boats have been restored and brought back to their former vivid beauty. The main patterns used include flowers, leaves, castles, bridges, horses, playing cards, scallops and striped bands of colour. Lettering is often part of the design, spelling out the name of the barge or its owner.

Free style

If the idea of living in a painted horse-drawn caravan or a canal boat sounds appealing but impractical, then why not settle for bringing some of the colour and atmosphere into your home? The bright colours are set against a dark background of either black, dark green or blue, and all the patterns are painted free-

hand. It is a true peasant painting style, which is great fun to do as it requires the type of loose, confident brush stroke that is best achieved after a glass or two of wine!

If you love the patterns but find the brilliance of the colours too overwhelming, try artificially fading them with a milky glaze of varnish tinted with a small amount of white. This effect will be more like an old sun-bleached painted caravan needing a fresh coat of paint. If this appeals, then you could take the illusion a stage further and rub back some of the paint to simulate wear and tear.

Small is beautiful

On a large scale this would be quite overpowering, but it is perfect for a small cubby-hole of a room, or just as part of a room. This project shows you how to make a pair of vibrantly patterned curtains to hang at your window. This window treatment will look equally good as the focal point in quite a plain room, as one of many patterns in a busy kitchen, or to add a touch of fantasy in a child's playroom. And a painted window-box filled with flowers outside the window is the perfect finishing touch.

PROJECT
Making felt appliqué curtains

YOU WILL NEED:

Cotton drill:
2 x double the
window width
x the height plus
100mm/4in

Felt in 4 other colours
(for example, green,
white, black, yellow)

Buttons for
decoration

Thread

Lining fabric – can be
cotton sheeting

Sewing machine

Rufflette tape for
curtain headings

Curtain rings

Fabric glue

A brush

COLOUR KEY

1 Leaf green
2 Scarlet
3 Deep sage green
4 Cream
5 Black

Felt decorations can give curtains a stylish, brightly coloured Romany look. Felt pattern shapes can be cut out and stuck down with glue. Although felt does not wash well, the colours are bright and will stay fresh-looking for a couple of years. The curtains are backed with a plain cotton lining.

Romany style has always included a variety of textiles – hand-dyed, woven, embroidered and appliquéed. The main pattern theme is a flower treated in a stylised way. These floral patterns are taken from Eastern European folk art and arranged in a typical way for decorating a long skirt or an apron.

TEMPLATE

Draw these patterns or copy them (enlarged to the desired size) and cut them out of thin paper. Then pin the patterns to felt and cut out the shapes.

HOW TO DO IT

These curtains are lined and headed with a simple tape and curtain rings. The decoration is glued in place with strong fabric glue but could also be fixed in place using a contrasting blanket stitch.

STEP 1 Cut out all the curtain and lining lengths. Draw the pattern shapes and cut them out of the coloured felt.

STEP 2 Arrange the pattern shapes on the background then glue each one in position (if you like hand-sewing then these can be edged in contrasting running stitch or blanket stitch).

STEP 3 Turn over a narrow hem on the lining side seams, then pin the linings on to the front of the curtains along the top edge, allowing roughly 25mm/1in for the seam. Stitch then turn the lining over onto the back and press the top seam flat.

STEP 4 Pin the heading tape to the lining about 25mm/1in from the top edge, then stitch it using the same colour thread as the felt curtain so that the stitching is invisible on the front.

STEP 5 Fit the curtain rings onto the heading tape and hang the curtains from the rail. Pin up the hem with the lining tucked into the seam, then loosely slip-stitch the hem (this can be done without taking the curtains down).

Tuscany

COLOUR
PALETTE

Tuscany in summer presents the perfect antidote to a grey winter spent in a city – the effect is instantaneous and unforgettable. Italy, like every other industrialised society, has moved away from old-style farming and many Italians choose new, problem-free housing with all mod cons over the tumbledown old farm buildings that fire the visitor's imagination. The restoration of farmhouses and villas in the Tuscan countryside has largely been undertaken by outsiders, for whom it was a case of 'love at first sight'.

It seems that another culture's rural lifestyle always has more appeal than one's own, doubly so when the weather is good. The outsiders have rescued what the locals would have thrown out in the name of progress, and craftsmen have found their traditional skills in great demand.

Tuscany has a treasury of art, architecture and culture in cities such as Florence and Siena, where the climate has helped to preserve its beauty. The colours of marble, earth and clay predominate, with the sun playing its part by fading fresh paint to blend seamlessly with the colours of older buildings.

The Tuscan climate is hot and dry, and houses are built of local stone with curved earthenware roof tiles. Windows have wooden shutters and the colouring of the buildings allows them to blend into the landscape.

Simple and functional

Inside, the houses have tiled floors and plastered walls painted in pink, shades of faded blue green or ochre yellow. There are no skirting boards, but the lower part of the walls are painted in a darker colour to hide the scuff marks made by the broom.

The small windows shield interiors from the scorching heat of the summer sun and the cold winter nights. Curtains are rare, but wooden shutters are fitted inside the windows, making it easy to block out the light during the afternoon rest hours. Windows ledges are tiled, and the broad bands surrounding windows and doorways are picked out in softly contrasting colours. The paint used in Tuscany is always limewash tinted with pigments. This is the perfect paint for the climate, and the chalky finish is essential for the authentic Tuscan look.

The furnishing style is simple and functional, as most entertaining takes place outside on the terrace. In Italy, furniture is often arranged against the walls rather than in the centre of a room to keep an open, spacious feeling. A few pieces of wooden furniture, some hand-painted ceramics, pot plants, Turkish rugs and table lamps are all in keeping with this style. Terracotta floor tiles are practical in an entrance hall and a kitchen, but are only suitable for living rooms in warmer climates. Polished floorboards and rugs look good and feel warmer underfoot.

The key to success is to keep it simple.

PROJECT
A painted wall finish

YOU WILL NEED:

Three shades of
chalk-finish paint

Large paintbrush
suitable for
colourwashing

Paint kettle

Masking tape

Long rule with
spirit level

Pencil for marking
the wall

The Tuscan decorating style is a simple one that uses weathered, textured and harmonious colour with no hard lines, startling primary colours or sharp contrasts. The look is not difficult to reproduce with Mediterranean paint that dries to a chalky finish. A slightly textured wall surface and colourwashed effect will intensify the Tuscan flavour, and the rough texture can be effectively applied with a special textured paint in a sand or farmhouse finish. The colour here is also used to surround the small key cupboard to add to the illusion of it being a shuttered window.

COLOUR KEY

1 Deep ochre

2 Dark terracotta

3 Deep purple

HOW TO DO IT

Keep the brush strokes fresh and energetic and use chalky water-based paint for an authentic Tuscan wall finish.

STEP 2 Measure 1m/3ft up from the floor and mark the wall at intervals. Draw a line along the length of the wall.

STEP 3 Place masking tape on the lower side of the 1m/3ft line and inside the border line.

STEP 1 Measure a border of 100mm/4in around any window, doorway or fitted feature, such as a cupboard, and mark this in pencil.

STEP 4 Dilute the paint and apply it to the lower wall and inside the inner border for the feature using random brushstrokes. Then leave it to dry.

STEP 5 Renew the tape and paint the top part of the wall and the outer border of the feature using the second, diluted paint. Peel off the tape and paint a freehand stripe in terracotta across the wall.

Moorish casbah

The Moorish style comes from the north of Africa where Morocco nestles between the Atlas mountains and the sea. This meeting point of African and Muslim culture has a rich artistic and cultural tradition. Islamic art and decoration is based on geometric patterns as the religion forbids the making of images. Houses are built around inner courtyards with plain, fortress-style exteriors; all of the decoration is on the inside. The courtyards are lined with open balconies, often with rows of columns and elaborate arches.

One of the most stunning features in Moorish homes is the tiling. Tiles are used on walls and floors to create elaborate interwoven shapes and patterns. The star features in most patterns, usually in the centre of a radiating trellis-work of star patterns. The main colours used are blue, white, black, pale green and terracotta. Colours are jewel-bright, whether on walls, tiles or woven in textiles.

Domes and arches

Other important features in Moorish design are domes, arches and water. Doorways are arched and windows are usually covered with decorative metal grilles. Walled rooftop terraces are the most popular place for evening entertaining. Walls are either topped off with stepped patterns or simply castellated and whitewashed to reflect the searing heat. Pools and fountains cool the courtyards, and date palms provide shade.

Pierced lanterns, leather pouffes, carved tea tables and intricately woven rugs are typical furnishings. Low couches are spread with rugs and silk cushions in all shapes and sizes. It is a style that encourages relaxation and a more exotic, sensual way of living.

Moroccan style is not expensive or beyond our reach thanks to the market culture which exists at the source in Morocco and in all major cities in Europe. The hippy trail led straight to Marrakesh in the late 1960s, and people soon discovered that they could finance their nomadic lifestyles by buying Moroccan goods and selling them back home to fund their next visit. As a result, the markets were flooded with folding tables, rugs, lanterns, trays and ceramics, many of which can still be picked up at reasonable prices in flea markets today. The ethnic decorating style which has been popular recently has brought a new wave of stylish Moroccan imports, but there are also plenty of beautiful and inexpensive pierced tin lanterns, sets of tea glasses, textiles and rugs on offer through homestyle stores and mail-order catalogues.

Exuberant palette

Travel guides for the area and books on Moorish architecture and interiors show this to be a rich mixture of sophisticated building and decoration enhanced by an exuberant ethnic palette.

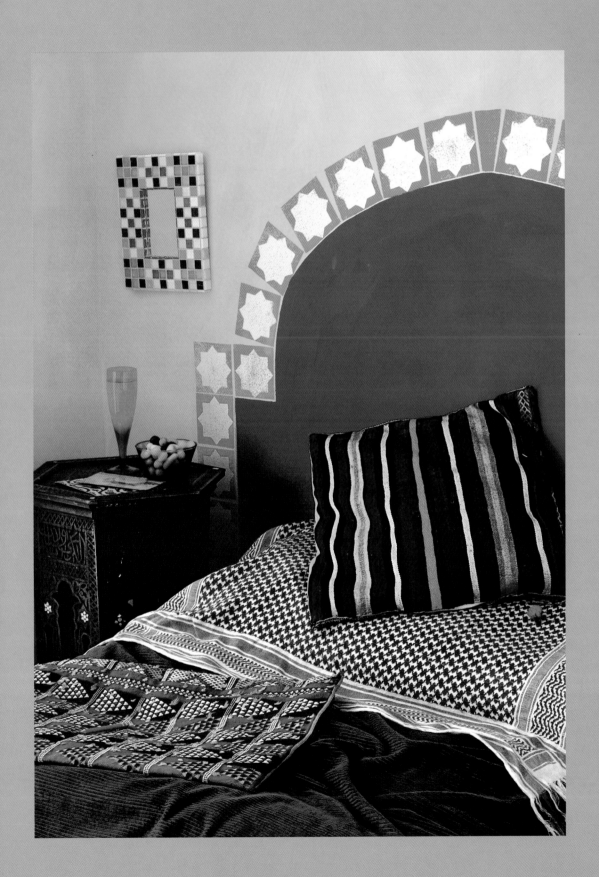

PROJECT
A painted arch bedhead

YOU WILL NEED:

Deep-blue chalky
finish paint

Pink paint

Deep terracotta paint

2 x 100mm/4in
squares of thick foam

Star pattern template

Scalpel

Spraymount

Brown wrapping
paper for the arch
template

Scissors

Chalk

Large brush to apply
main colour

Small paintbrush
for edges

COLOUR KEY

1 Tangerine

2 Deep ultramarine

3 Palest lemon

Turn your bedroom into a scene from *A Thousand and One Nights* by painting the walls a warm pink stone colour and painting a typically Moorish arch at the bedhead in deep ultramarine blue with a stamped tile surround. Enhance the casbah atmosphere with metal lanterns, candles, urns and striped woven textiles. All the other colours in the room should be rich and warm so that the effect is one of looking up at an inky blue Moroccan night sky. If this effect appeals to you, why not go one step further and paint a distant sickle moon and stars on the blue arch shape?

TEMPLATE

Draw the star pattern so that it fits neatly into a 100mm/4in square following the method shown in the diagram.

HOW TO DO IT

This arched bedhead does not take long to paint, and the stamped tiles are simple, bold and effective.

STEP 1 Enlarge and draw one half of the arch pattern onto the brown parcel paper, either in sections on a photocopier or by squaring up. Cut it out and spray a light coating of Spraymount on one side.

STEP 2 Stick this onto the wall and draw the shape with chalk, then flip the template over and repeat these steps to create a complete arch.

STEP 3 Enlarge the star pattern to 80mm/3¼in wide and stick the pattern onto one of the foam squares. Carefully cut out the shape to the depth of about 15mm/⅝in. Cut outwards from the middle every time. Peel off the background to 15mm/⅝in, leaving a star-shaped stamp.

STEP 4 Paint the arch in deep blue, using the small brush for a neat finish around the edges.

STEP 5 Put some of the terracotta paint onto a plate and coat the square tile stamp. Stamp a tile border around the edge of the arch, leaving the top triangle for now. Allow to dry.

STEP 6 Now coat the star stamp in pink and place one star in every tile shape. Cut a foam stamp in a triangle shape to fill the gap at the top and on each side where the arch meets the straight supporting column. Fill in the gaps with this stamp using the terracotta colour.

India

The subcontinent of India is a huge country of many distinct characters. The Buddhist north is mountainous with a cold climate, and to the west lie the farmlands and deserts of Rajasthan and Gujarat, which border the Arabian Sea. The Hindu south has the hottest climate and the most relaxed lifestyle, and here the economy is based around the traditional creative industries of textile printing and carving. The east has the River Ganges, jungles, mangrove swamps and Calcutta, the most overpopulated city in India.

There is no such thing as one Indian style, but one thing all the regions have in common is that they mix brilliant colours in ways that break all the Western rules defining 'good taste' and colour combining! The result is vibrant, energising and uniquely Indian. Colours are flung together with great confidence, and their impact is stunning. Different areas of India are famous for their skills in specific crafts such as embroidery, textile printing, pottery or carpet weaving, but there is no area where most of these traditional skills are not practised anyway.

Brilliant work

It is clear from the dress, homes and jewellery of the craftspeople who produce these items that they have a genuine love for the patterns, colours and motifs they reproduce, even though they are poorly paid for the work that they do. Most of the work is produced for the home market. Houses in cities are painted in brilliant colours; temples are adorned with carvings and bronze castings, and each festival generates a hive of industry producing all the necessary deities, offerings and accessories needed for a proper celebration.

Seeking out the style

Many of the styles we recognise as our own have their origins in India. The paisley shawl, floral chintz, Madras check, Provençal prints and damask cottons all came from India. Several charities now have Fair Trade arrangements with communities of craftspeople in India who supply goods directly for sale in their high street shops, so it is really easy to buy genuine handmade accessories, textiles and ornaments to give a room the right feel.

The sari stores found in the local shops of Asian communities sell lengths of fabric ranging from plain vibrant muslins for everyday wear to the finest exquisitely embroidered cloth for wedding saris. Sari lengths are ideal for draping over curtain poles at windows or as exotic drapes for a four-poster bed.

Most paint companies produce vibrant colour ranges. Choose the mainstream emulsion paints for children's rooms where these brilliant colour schemes will always find an appreciative audience; or buy a Mediterranean-style paint that dries to leave an authentic powdery bloom.

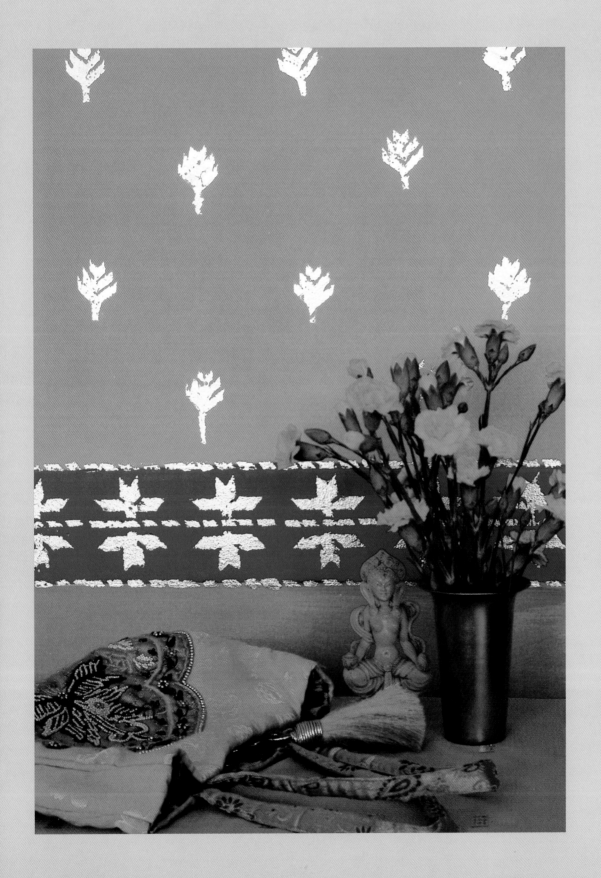

PROJECT
Bindi stamps and a border stamp

YOU WILL NEED:

High density foam

Scalpel

Copies of the patterns

Spraymount

Size (special glue)

Small foam roller

Plumb line marked at 300mm/12in intervals

2 or more packs of gold leaf – (the squares can be cut in half with scissors or a scalpel, to avoid waste)

Very few textiles escape having some extra form of decoration beyond colour dye in India. It is as if they simply cannot resist adding another pattern, thread or ornament.

These little teardrop shapes are inspired by the decorative marks which Indian women paint or apply to their foreheads, called *bindi*.

The shape is stamped onto the wall using a clear glue called gold size, then when it is almost dry a sheet of gold leaf is rubbed over it. The result is a gleaming gold shape. The pattern for the border is larger and can be applied either in the same way or with a bright pink paint colour as shown here.

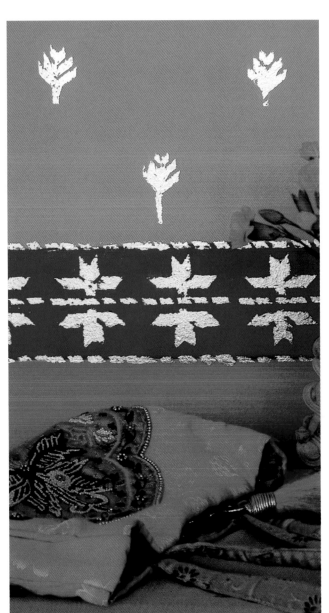

COLOUR KEY

1 Deep lavender

2 Lilac

3 Lavender grey

4 Palest lemon

5 Apricot

TEMPLATE

These are the actual size patterns for the foam stamps and can be traced from the book. Use thin paper that will be easily cut through when you make the stamps.

HOW TO DO IT

Foam stamps can be made from any firm foam, but cutting needs to be done slowly and accurately to get the best effect.

STEP 1 Make copies of the patterns and stick them on the foam. Cut them out carefully, using a scalpel. Practise cutting on an off-cut to judge how much pressure is needed. Cut at an angle so the base of the pattern is wider than the top; this makes the stamp stronger.

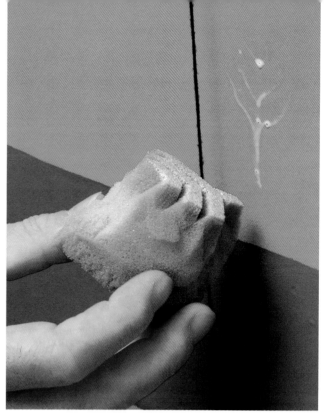

STEP 2 Put 1 tablespoon of size on a plate and run the foam roller through it. Coat the *bindi* and stamp it onto the wall at 600mm/25in intervals using the plumb line as a guide. Stamp the next row, starting 300mm/12in from the ceiling to make a half-drop pattern.

STEP 3 Take a sheet of gold leaf with its backing sheet and rub it gently onto the stamped size. The leaf will cling to the size, but easily brush away from the surrounding wall. Don't worry if the motifs are not sharp-edged – this is typical of the hand-blocked style.

STEP 4 Apply size to the border stamp and repeat the pattern along the deep violet band. Complete the whole length of the wall, then apply the sheets of gold leaf. Brush away the excess, then burnish the gold with a soft cloth.

African

The African continent is one of many contrasts, divided in half at the equator by a band of heavy forests. To the north is the massive Sahara desert with the huge countries of Egypt and Sudan. Egypt is one of the great ancient civilisations, whose past is well documented compared to the other African civilisations. In contrast, there are still tribes who lead a Stone Age existence as hunter-gatherers deep in the equatorial forests, or as nomadic huntsmen in the Southern deserts.

East Africa borders the Indian Ocean and the Red Sea, and trade with India and the Arab countries over the centuries has made North East Africa more Arab in style than African. There are white domed buildings, minarets, date palms and bustling markets. Southern Africa has the grasslands, lakes, mountains and semi-deserts, and wildlife, and people traditionally lived off the land as herdsmen and farmers. Much of Africa's rich heritage of art, crafts and architecture was undermined by colonisation, and only recently has a pride in true African style re-emerged.

Updated traditions

The textiles of West Africa are amazingly varied. Traditional fabric patterns were tie-dyed or patterned using the mud-resist technique, and coloured with indigo or other organic plant dyes. Modern dyes are used now, with mixtures of old and new designs. Some of the most interesting feature objects such as bicycles or clocks as design motifs set within traditional border patterns. Utility objects such as baskets, rugs or pottery remain unchanged. Authentic African goods including textiles and household goods have

been added to beadwork, trinkets and wood carvings for the export market. The abstract patterns and simple shapes fit in well with contemporary interiors.

African colour

The Southern African colour palette comes from the earth. Red ochre, yellow, burnt orange and black dominate, with any other available colour used to riotous effect. In some places telephone wires are split open and the multi-colour wires used to weave baskets; in others tin cans are recycled to make storage trunks, lamps and toys.

Creating an authentic African-style room should not be difficult or expensive. The look is simple and relies on a few well-chosen objects, shapes and colours. The walls are roughly textured and painted in bands of colour, dark at the bottom and light above. Patterns are loosely geometric and rhythmic. There are specialist stores that deal in African furniture and crafts; baskets, masks, woven wall hangings and soapstone carvings are always on sale in Oxfam's stores and it is always worth exploring flea markets and junk shops for stools, tables or curios.

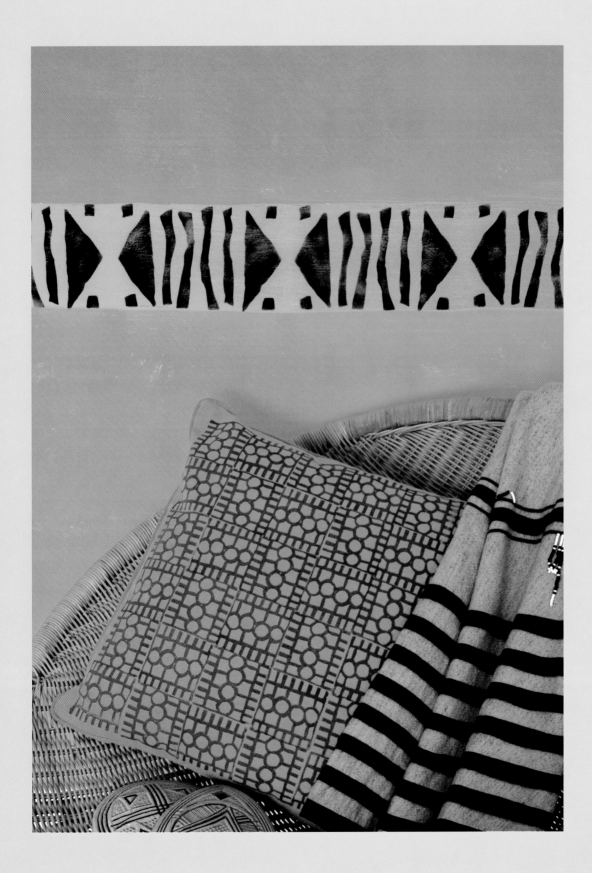

PROJECT
African walls

YOU WILL NEED:

Earthy orange, golden
yellow, mud brown
and warm terracotta
paints in sample size
for stencilling

Matt black emulsion
paint (small tin)

Short-pile roller

Broad paintbrush

40mm/1½in
paintbrush

Long rule and
spirit level

Pencil

Stencil card

Spraymount

Scalpel

Short, fat
stencil brush

The walls in African homes have undulating surfaces that are pitted and rough in places and shiny smooth in others. Smooth walls may need roughing up a bit to achieve the African look. There are several ways to do this. The least expensive is to apply a skim coat of plaster with a wooden trowel, but this is something of a specialist job. A thin, uneven coat of filler can be applied, with a plastering trowel or a large brush, having mixed it 50:50 into white emulsion paint; or special effect paint, applied with a short-pile roller and given random criss-cross strokes with a decorating brush.

COLOUR KEY

1 Earthy orange

2 Golden yellow

3 Mud brown

4 Warm terracotta

TEMPLATE
This stencil imitates stick printed patterns, so keep the lines irregular when you cut it out.

HOW TO DO IT

Stencilling is easy and effective so long as you use Spraymount to hold the stencil in place and remember to use only the smallest amount of paint on your brush.

STEP 1 Measure and mark the wall at 750mm/30in and 1m/3ft height at 1m/3ft intervals around the walls and draw guidelines for the three bands.

STEP 2 Paint the top and bottom parts of the wall first and leave to dry.

STEP 3 Paint the dividing band with your chosen emulsion. Paint the lines free-hand using the narrower brush along the edges and filling in with the broader brush.

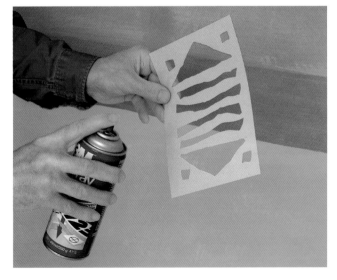

STEP 4 Cut out the stencil pattern and apply a small amount of Spraymount to the back of it.

STEP 5 Stencil the pattern in the centre band in your chosen colour.

Miami pastel brights

Miami Beach at the tip of Florida has a style all of its own. The resort was built between the 1920s and 1940s in the Art Deco style, which was popular in New York and Chicago, but in Miami they gave the look a unique twist by choosing a very different range of colours for their buildings. In Miami the buildings were painted with bright tropical pinks, sunny yellows, purples, blues and greens. The colours were not primaries but bright pastel ice-cream colours, perfect for a holiday town.

The buildings echoed the shape of streamlined ocean liners, with the main body of the building painted white and colour used to highlight the horizontal banding. For a while Miami was the most glamorous holiday destination, but it fell on hard times in the late 1950s. In the 1980s a massive renovation plan was set in motion, and now Miami outshines its former glory. The buildings are freshly painted and are a little brighter, with less white and more entire buildings painted bright colours; the chrome is polished and neon signs light up the night. The interiors are decorated in a similar style, using colours to stress the geometric devices in the design such as columns, stepped parapets and windows with narrow horizontal glazing bars. Also synonymous with Miami are palm trees, tropical flowers, nautical themes, flamingos and unrestrained elegance.

Art Deco Miami-style

Miami is now one of the world's top holiday resorts, and its stylish hotels and boulevards are favourite locations for films and fashion photography. Creating your own piece of South Beach (SoBe) should not be too hard

because a distinctive colour scheme will do most of the work for you. Look out for one or two genuine Art Deco pieces of furniture, either from specialist dealers or flea markets.

Miami used Art Deco shapes but applied its own colour scheme – you can do the same with bright pastel upholstery. If you have no luck finding original furniture, buy a plain sofa with a streamlined shape and dress it up with contrasting cushions piped in Miami colours.

A touch of fun

Neon lighting is very much a part of the Miami look, and a pair of coloured neon tubes would add an authentic glow at night. These can be bought as coloured sheaths to fit over standard tubes. Chrome wall or table lights will also fit in well, and there are plenty of good reproduction Art Deco lights around.

Miami has a fun side, and if this appeals to you then a fake flamingo or two and a few stylized sunset pictures are a must! In Miami, the sun shines all year and most residents are on permanent vacation. Adopt this style at home so that, even if work occupies the day, every evening will feel like a holiday.

PROJECT
Miami deco walls

YOU WILL NEED:

Background colour
(choose one of the
three below) to
apply to all wall
surfaces first

Pink, yellow and sea
green paint

Pencil

Long rule

Spirit level

Plumb line

Paintbrush

Roller and tray

Small foam roller
and tray

Decorator's
masking tape

The geometric and streamlined shapes associated with Art Deco can be used mural-style, drawn onto a wall and painted using the Miami palette of tropical bright pastels. The most important lines to emphasise are the horizontals, which should wrap around the room in smooth streamlined stripes. Vertical columns topped off with stepped parapets can be painted around doorways or windows.

Miami is very style-conscious but fun is also high on the agenda, so use the basic shapes and colours but feel free to interpret the style in your own way.

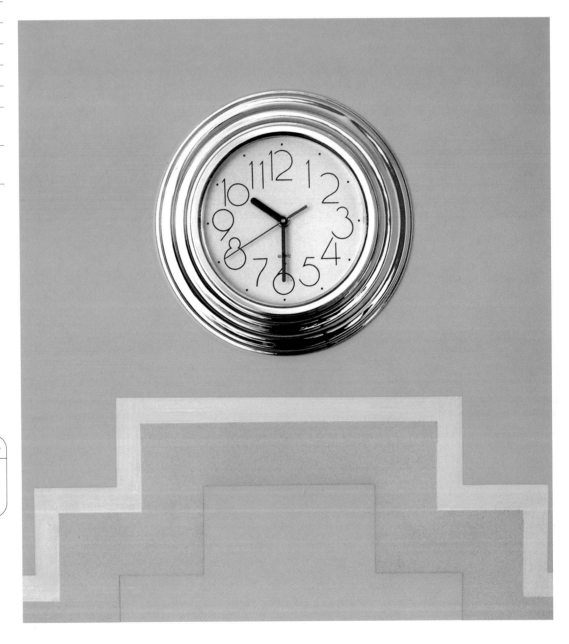

COLOUR KEY

1 Lemon curd

2 Deep rose

3 Aqua blue

HOW TO DO IT

Wrapping your walls with these bands of Miami colour will liven up any room. It's fun, but don't rush it as the paint needs to be dry before you apply the tape.

STEP 1 Draw the streamlining stripes by measuring up from the floor, and marking then drawing pencil lines. Check them with the spirit level.

STEP 2 Run masking tape around the outside edge of the lines.

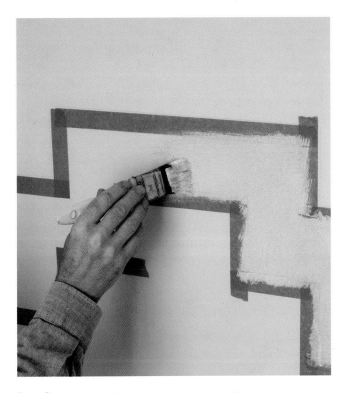

STEP 3 Paint the bands of colour inside the masking tape.

STEP 4 Leave until almost dry, then peel off the tape.

Industrial modern

The industrial look is one that was born out of necessity, when young people in big cities like New York, Paris and London went looking for places to live and found themselves priced out of the market. The empty properties that attracted their attention were dockland warehouses and abandoned factories whose business had long since closed down or moved out of town to escape the traffic-clogged streets. The buildings presented an opportunity for a whole new way of living, and loft style was born.

One of the most essential aspects of industrial modern style is to retain as much of the fabric of the original building and any specialist associated material as possible. A large winch with an iron hook, for instance, would be seen as sculptural and retained, as would a metal staircase, steel shutters or a ventilation shaft. The idea is to retain the best of the building's original character, but also to make it work as a comfortable home.

Fabulous fittings

Once the factory and warehouse spaces had been colonised, the next step was to make use of factory fittings, office furniture and items of industrial scale that could be converted for use in the home. Galvanised iron shelving, movable storage units on hefty rubber casters and cafeteria tables were put to immediate use, and aluminium waste bins, metal filing cabinets, catering ovens and sets of lockers began appearing on the pages of magazines. Floors were covered with aluminium sheeting or painted with industrial paints; brickwork was exposed, and scaffolding poles were used to create mezzanine sleeping decks in the middle of vast open spaces.

Lofts and warehouses have now moved up to the top end of the market – but the industrial modern style is here to stay. Aluminium flooring, stainless steel units and catering ovens are readily available. There are aluminium and steel acrylic paints that will make any surface look like cool metal, and a range of textured wall covering that looks just like factory flooring. Metal storeroom-type shelving, track lighting and bare concrete used for seating, tables, shelving supports and planters are all a part of this pared-down style.

'Islands of comfort' are another vital ingredient – cool hard surfaces look fabulous, but everyone needs to curl up and feel warm and comfortable as well. These comfort zones are furnished with generous leather sofas, soft mohair or lamb's-wool throws, deep pile rugs and low coffee tables. Even in a vast space, clever lighting can create a sense of intimacy if kept low and concentrated by using floor and table lamps to cast warm pools of light. Use the same basic concepts to create an industrial modern style in any room – keep the style utilitarian and the space cool, open and uncluttered, but be sure to include soft areas for comfort and indulgence.

PROJECT
Breeze-block shelving

YOU WILL NEED:

6 breeze blocks

2 x 350mm x 2m
x 20mm/14in x 6ft
x ¾in planks

Primer

Matt black paint

Paintbrush

Concrete breeze blocks have replaced bricks as the basic construction material in most new houses these days. They are regular-sized, strong and inexpensive, but they don't make beautiful looking walls, so bricks are still used as a facing material. The rough grey texture of the blocks takes on a more sculptural quality when taken out of context and used indoors as shelf supports.

The planks used here are painted black wood but other materials would also look good. Glass, steel mesh or galvanised zinc are all very much a part of the industrial modern style.

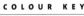

COLOUR KEY

1 Mushroom brown
2 Mid-grey
3 Palest lemon
4 Pale mushroom

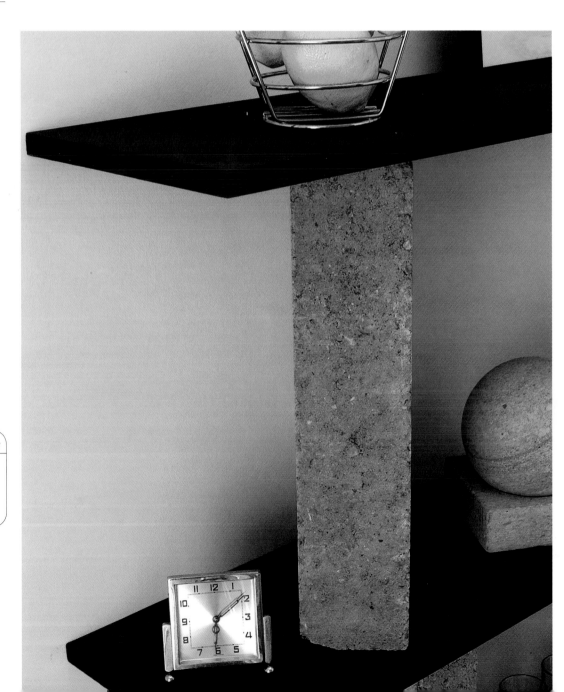

HOW TO DO IT

The sculptural style of this shelving unit relies on the positioning of the breeze blocks. Use a set square to align each one at the correct angle.

STEP 1 Apply a coat of primer to the shelving planks. Leave to dry, then apply two coats of black paint.

STEP 2 Space two base breeze blocks to stand 60mm/2½in from the wall, 500mm/20in apart, angled at 45° to the wall. Stand the first shelf on top with 250mm/10in overlap at each end.

STEP 3 Place two more blocks on the shelf above the lower ones, this time angled at 90°, the narrow side facing forwards.

STEP 4 Stand the second shelf on top, again with 250mm/10in overlap at each end, and position the final two blocks angled at 45°. Put the third shelf on top. Note: this shelving unit should only be used in rooms with solid floors and where it is unlikely to be knocked.

Urban minimalist

COLOUR
PALETTE

The key elements for this look are open space, good colour and only a few well-designed pieces of furniture. Floors are left bare with either painted or waxed floorboards. Ornaments are out – instead, choose really stylish utility objects which are sculptural in their own right. We all need radiators, but the urban minimalist goes for fabulous columns, swirls or ladder-style 'rads'. Everything makes a style statement, and for this look you really do have to maintain a disciplined attitude to tidiness, because clutter is definitely out.

The furniture can be from any period so long as it is in good condition and has a design pedigree – some of the most contemporary looking chairs and loungers were actually designed in the 1920s by the famous community of designers at the Bauhaus in Germany. Chairs from any of the key decades in the last century can be reupholstered in plain contemporary colours to flatter their shape. Brand new technology sits comfortably alongside retro pieces, so long as the good design ethos remains paramount.

Urban colour

Light interiors are always enhanced when a good proportion of white is used, as it reflects and doubles the room's natural light. Leave windows bare when possible and paint window frames and surrounds white. If the windows are small then create the impression of bigger windows by painting a broad white border beyond the frames and below the sill down to floor level, which will create the impression of full length windows. Folding wooden blinds look wonderful, but if they are likely to blow the budget choose plain white blinds instead.

The urban minimalist look consists of just a few equally important elements, and colour is one of them. Consider the room's function and any existing colour that appears in furnishings, paintings or accessories when choosing a wall colour.

Adding accents

A meditative lavender or pale powder blue creates a relaxing atmosphere in a sitting room, and pale mushroom brown looks good with white and deeper browns, especially if bright colours such as spring green or red are used for upholstery. Just one or two permanent colours are needed, and others can be added as colour accents with cushions, vases or flower arrangements.

Fresh flowers are very much a part of the urban minimalist look, and a whole new style of floristry has emerged to complement it. Single variety arrangements or indoor plants are favoured, such as vibrantly red or orange dahlias in tall glass tubes; rows of pink orchids growing in moss-covered containers; zinc tubs planted with white marguerite daisies or a huge earthenware pot filled with tall wild grasses.

PROJECT
Making a bolster cushion

COLOUR
PALETTE

YOU WILL NEED:

A bolster cushion pad

Rough silk fabric in a bold colour – enough to wrap around the body of the bolster plus two circles for the ends. Cut them to allow for a 15mm/⅝in seam

Matching thread

Piping cord (cut a strip of fabric and fold it over the cord, then stitch close to the cord using the zipper foot, and clip along the seam allowance so the cord bends easily into a curve)

A zip to fit length

Scissors

Pins

Sewing machine

A bright silk bolster cushion on a sofa or chair can be used to add an accent of colour to the room. Bolsters are long, firm tubular cushions whose shape and proportions suit the minimalist look. They were a popular feature of the design-conscious Regency and Biedermeier styles in the 19th century, and Le Corbusier's famous leather and chrome lounger has a bolster neckrest, which certainly confers it with top design credentials.

The secret of success is to take the sewing slowly so that you keep turning the fabric in a smooth curve.

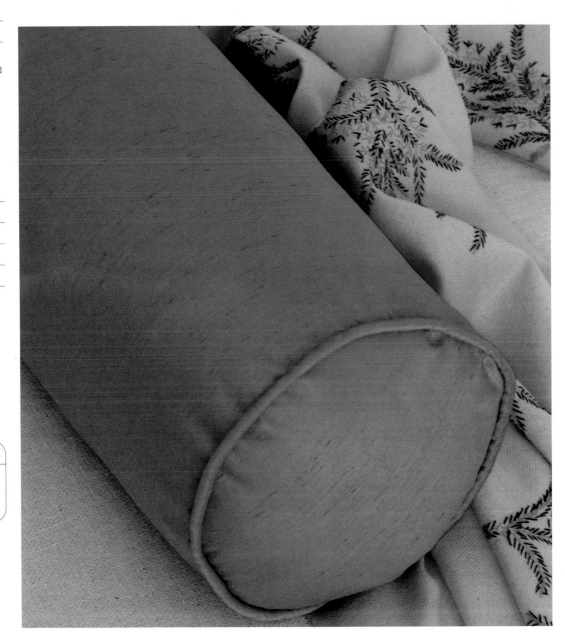

COLOUR KEY	
1	Soft emerald
2	Fawn
3	Deep golden yellow

HOW TO DO IT

Fit a zipper foot to the sewing machine so that you can stitch up close to the piping and the zip.

STEP 1 Turn over a small hem and stitch the zip into the seam of the main body fabric. Undo the zip so you can work on the cover.

STEP 2 Sew the piping onto the round ends before you stitch them to the main body.

STEP 3 Snip out 10mm/³⁄₈in notches every 30mm/1¼in around the end pieces. Pin the ends in place and stitch them using the zipper foot to get close up to the piping cord.

STEP 4 Press the seams lightly and turn the right side out. Fit the cushion pad inside and close the zip.

Index

Acknowledgements

The publishers would like to thank the following for use of copyright material:

Laura Ashley Limited: pp. 28, 45, 49(t), 50, 51(b), 52, 53(b), 53(br).

Elizabeth Whiting Associates: 3, 6, 7, 9, 13, 15(m), 15(tr), 18, 19, 20(t), 20(b), 21(t), 21(b), 22, 25, 29(t), 29(b), 48, 49(b), 51(t).

b = bottom, br = bottom right, m = middle, tr = top right, t = top.